Surviving Celibacy

by
Stephen Fierbaugh

...when there is no "Happily Ever After"...

Surviving Celibacy

© 2010 Stephen Fierbaugh
International Standard Book Number: 978-0-578-04608-2

Cover Design: Miss Lee Fierbaugh

This work is distributed under the Creative Commons "Attribution-ShareAlike 3.0 United States" license. Limited duplication is permitted.

You are free to:

to Share – to copy, distribute, display, and perform the work

to Remix – to make derivative works

Under the following conditions:

Attribution. You must attribute the work in the manner specified by the author or licensor (but not in any way that suggests that they endorse you or your use of the work).

Share Alike. If you alter, transform, or build upon this work, you may distribute the resulting work only under the same, similar or a compatible license.

For any reuse or distribution, you must make clear to others the license terms of this work. Any of the above conditions can be waived if you get permission from the copyright holder. Apart from the remix rights granted under this license, nothing in this license impairs or restricts the author's moral rights.

Your fair use and other rights are in no way affected by the above.
This is a human-readable summary of the Legal Code (the full license), located at "http://creativecommons.org/licenses/by-sa/3.0/us/legalcode".

Publishing History
First Edition, 2009
(Published as *Celibacy Sucks But We're Not Alone!*)
Second Edition 2010

*To all the ladies who said, "No." Thank you.
I learned a little from each of you.*

Preface

This book is a rarity. There are shelves full of books for Christian singles on how to find a mate or how to behave before finding a mate. A few are actually pretty good; most are bad. Nearly all are written by married people.

There is very little guidance for singles like us who have figured out two very important personal facts:

1. Marriage may or may not ever occur, but it sure isn't going to happen any time soon.
2. Time is passing.

There are no "how-to's" for singles trying to figure out how to live a godly Christian life in their thirties, forties, and later, when everything in both society and the church tells us we are failures.

Since nobody else is giving us instruction, let us turn to the one source of wisdom that does deal with our issues: the Bible. As much as possible, this book just points out what the Word of God says. What it says – and doesn't say – will probably surprise you.

We follow this journey together. This book will not be full of platitudes from people who have never walked in your shoes.

A Note on Scripture

Throughout it all, Scripture will be our guide.

We are blessed with a number of English translations of the Bible. Occasionally, they differ in trivial ways for specific passages. In the vast majority of cases, it is a moot point because the differences are irrelevant to the meaning of the passage. Be forewarned that some of the key passages that we will be dealing with, 1st Corinthians 7 and Ephesians 5:3, do in fact vary somewhat between translations in ways that are significant to our purposes. The original Greek is clear, but it isn't always easy to tell to which object pronouns are referring.

This book, for the most part, uses the New English Translation (NET), not because of its handling of these specific passages, but rather because of its voluminous translation notes explaining why a passage was translated the way it was and what are other viable alternate translations. Check out other quality translations such as the New American Standard and the New International Version, as well. While the points we are studying are clearer in some translations than others, any of these translations is suitable for study.

Contents

Preface..1
A Note on Scripture..3
Prologue: Am I a eunuch?..7
Chapter 1: So am I a eunuch?..9
Chapter 2: Balderdash!...11
Chapter 3: Guaranteed Spouse?..14
Chapter 4: Divorce..16
Chapter 5: Dietrich Bonhoeffer..22
Chapter 6: Depression..28
Chapter 7: Betsie and Corrie ten Boom...32
Chapter 8: Hatred and Hurt..38
Chapter 9: Meddling (Theirs)...46
Chapter 10: Meddling (Ours)...50
Chapter 11: Lust..52
Chapter 12: Masturbation...60
Chapter 13: Homosexuality..68
Chapter 14: C. S. Lewis..72
Chapter 15: The 40 Year Old Virgin..78
Chapter 16: Rich Mullins..80
Chapter 17: No hope?...84
Chapter 18: Coveting, Envy, and Bitterness.....................................86
Chapter 19: Amy Carmichael...90
Chapter 20: Failure...94
Chapter 21: Loneliness...98
Chapter 22: Ellie Grant Devore..104
Chapter 23: Stop waiting and live life!..110
Appendix A: For Pastors..114
Chapter 24: Just how many singles are there?................................116
    The Male/Female Disparity..117
    Why should you care?...118
    Why do singles need their own ministry?...............................118
Chapter 25: The anatomy of your singles.......................................120
    Divorce...120
    Loneliness..120
    Depression and other mental issues..121
    Handicaps, excess weight, & ugliness.....................................121
    Substance abuse and similar issues...122

 Despair..122
 Giving & finances..122
 Commitment & free time..123
 Beware S.A.D.!..123
Chapter 26: Teaching Singles...126
 Find me a mate!..127
 It's not all about sex..128
 Raise their expectations..130
 Everyone needs to feel loved...130
 Stealth Dating...130
 What about the meat market?..132
 The Creepiness Equation..133
 Warning: It's your ministry but their family.............................134
Chapter 27: Meddling (Yours)..135
Conclusion: Lead your sheep!..139
Appendix B: Study Guide...141
 Shadowlands (C. S. Lewis)...142
  Popcorn Break!..142
 The Hiding Place (Betsie & Corrie ten Boom).........................144
  Popcorn Break!..144
 The Story of Amy Carmichael...146
  Popcorn Break!..146
 Bonhoeffer: Agent of Grace...148
  Popcorn Break!..148
About the Author..151

Prologue: Am I a eunuch?

> *He said to them, "Not everyone can accept this statement, except those to whom it has been given. For there are some eunuchs who were that way from birth, and some who were made eunuchs by others, and some who became eunuchs for the sake of the kingdom of heaven. The one who is able to accept this should accept it."* (Matthew 19:11-12 NET)

In Jesus' day, all respectable women were married and men were almost always married unless they were castrated, but today there are many godly people of both sexes who – for a variety of reasons – are not married.

If you're reading this book, you are probably between 25 and 50. You're not married. And you've figured out that your prospects of getting married any time soon are not really that hot. In fact, you may be starting to wonder if Jesus was talking about you; are you going to be single the rest of your life? Are you going to end up an "old maid" (don't you hate that term)? And the prospect scares you to death.

I know. I'm in the same boat. I looked around and could not find anyone to tell me how this plays out in today's society. How does a godly man or woman age gracefully into their late thirties and older without being married?

Actually, a pretty good question before we get to that point is simply, "Can we?" Is it possible for a Christian to remain unmarried their entire life in today's society and still be a productive member of the Church?

Prologue: Am I a eunuch?

The reason we have to ask is that there aren't a lot of older Christian singles who make suitable role models.

So, is it possible? Well, it certainly isn't easy. That much is obvious. We're going to go out on a limb and state as an axiom for this book that it may not be easy, but it is possible. While that may be a statement of faith more than experience, Jesus and Paul both talk about them.

And the history of the Church is full of role models! The writer of Hebrews told us, *"Remember your leaders, who spoke God's message to you; reflect on the outcome of their lives and imitate their faith."* (Hebrews 13:7 NET)

Some of the greatest Church leaders of the last hundred years were unmarried or married very late in life. And their stories are amazing! Intermingled with our examination of the issues, we will be examining some of their lives for inspiration. Movies have been made about four of them, and there is a movie study guide in Appendix B.

Since you are probably as tired as I am of sitting through sermons and lessons by people who haven't got a clue what you are really struggling with, Appendix A is specifically for Church leaders and teachers.

Chapter 1: So am I a eunuch?

> *Not everyone can accept this statement, except those to whom it has been given. For there are some eunuchs who were that way from birth, and some who were made eunuchs by others, and some who became eunuchs for the sake of the kingdom of heaven. The one who is able to accept this should accept it.* (Matthew 19:11-12 NET)

Well, let's look at what Jesus actually said... The context of this statement was a question about divorce, as we will study a little later. But let's get this big question out of the way up front because most of us are scared to death of it.

Jesus says some people are born with no desire for sex. Others are made that way by men; back then he meant castration, but it's also true that some men and women have seen how nasty their parents' marriages were and honestly don't feel any inclination towards a spouse. And a few choose not to marry for the sake of their Christian ministry; there are some wonderful Christian missionaries who, if they were in America, would meet a mate, but simply do not have the opportunity because of their ministry lifestyle.

This is some of Jesus' toughest teaching. He understands intimately what he is talking about because he is in that third group. Jesus knows that it is a hard, hard teaching. He both precedes and follows it with a warning that it is not for anyone except those who find themselves in this situation and can accept it. Paul says the same when he addresses our situation: *"To the unmarried and widows I say that it is best for them to remain as I am. But if they do not have self-control, let them get married. For it is better to marry than to burn with sexual desire."* (1st Corinthians 7:8-9 NET)[1]

So both places in Scripture where we are talked about, God clearly surrounds it with caveats. Some of this will be dealt with in more detail in chapter 3, on divorce, but for now put your heart at ease.

If you have no desire for marriage, or find yourself in a circumstance where you cannot marry, or it is more prudent for you to remain single, do so. Don't let anyone push you into it and don't feel like a second-class citizen; you are a full blown member of the Church just like anyone else. You are going to reap dynamite rewards in heaven.

If you have a deep desire for a spouse & family, and the circumstance arises where you may marry, do so. Don't let anyone push you into denying what God has allowed.

Both the preceding paragraphs require wisdom in their application. Some of us have pasts such that it would be only prudent to go cautiously and seek godly counsel. But put your heart at rest on this topic. This message comes straight from God: *"If you marry, you have not sinned."* (1st Corinthians 7:28 NET)

This book is about living your Christian life as a single, not about finding a godly mate. The bookshelves are full of books on that topic. We'll only be dealing with marriage and remarriage incidental to our discussion of our Christian walk.

---

[1] If you are following along in your own Bible, good! You might as well bookmark 1st Corinthians 7. We're going to be coming back to this chapter again and again.

Chapter 2: Balderdash!

- "If he must think of the medical side of chastity, feed him the grand lie which we have made the English humans believe, that physical exercise in excess and consequent fatigue are specially favorable to this virtue. How they can believe this, in face of the notorious lustfulness of sailors and soldiers, may well be asked. But we used the schoolmasters to put the story about..." Advice from Screwtape to Wormwood, letter 18, *The Screwtape Letters*, C. S. Lewis

- *Examine all things; hold fast to what is good.* 1 Thessalonians 5:21 NET

One of the most useful skills we can have as singles in our mental and spiritual tool-chest is a good Balderdash Detector. This may be particularly useful while reading books on singleness and celibacy! ;-)

Balderdash is, simply put, nonsense. Information which isn't true. A statement that sounds good and is put forward with authority, but just doesn't actually jibe with reality.

There is a lot of balderdash directed at singles by people in positions of authority, both Christian and secular. Usually they are learned people who are talking about something of which they have little or no direct knowledge or study. The teacher, professor, or pastor saying it may honestly believe that it is true. But it isn't, and often a little critical

Balderdash!

thinking and applied logic will reveal gaping fallacies.

C. S. Lewis skewers one common balderdash in a good example. As we will discover in a later chapter, Lewis knew a thing or two about singleness. This teaching that physical exercise will reduce libido or lust is called "sublimation", and it is taught by a wide swath of authorities, including Gnosticism, Freudian psychoanalysis, eastern religions, communism, and contemporary evangelicalism; just about everyone, in fact, except actual medical scientists. I remember being taught it in Bible college. Yet Lewis simply applies a little skepticism and asks, "Does this make sense? Does it jibe with what I know of the real world?" Balderdash!

"Two singles sharing a house must be gay." Balderdash!

"Two singles spending a lot of time together must be in a romantic relationship." Balderdash!

"All the good ones are married or gay." Balderdash! What am I? What are you?

"You'll get married as soon as you stop making it your idol." Balderdash! So now Paul and Jeremiah were not spiritual enough?

"Two singles in a romantic relationship must be having sex." Balderdash!

"There is someone special waiting for everyone." Balderdash! Sorry, this is mathematically impossible. There are over 4 million more females than males in the US[2]; 7 million more if we discount the 2% of men who are behind bars. (This one is so pernicious that we'll cover it further in the next chapter.)

"After 40, it's too late." Balderdash! We're going to look at some singles who proved this startlingly wrong, both romantically and in Christian service.

"All singles are divorced." Balderdash! 60% of single adults have never married. 25% are divorced, and 15% are widowed[3]. (This one is

---

2 Factfinder.census.gov: DP-1 General Demographic Characteristics 2008 Population Estimates
3 Ibid.

Balderdash!

a twisted distortion of the fact that most of us have been impacted by divorce, whether or not our own, so we'll look at it in the chapter after next.)

Sex is clearly a popular subgenre of balderdash. There is so much misinformation out there, propounded by all manner of secular and religious "experts", that it's hard to know who and what to believe. In reality, human sexuality is so diverse, broad, and complex, that there are few, if any, absolute truisms which can be drawn about sexual behavior.

As we read or listen to anything, compare the teaching to Scripture and common sense. The Bible has been tested and tried by two millennium of Christians. Its descriptions of human nature are clear and trustworthy. God wants us to use our judgment in filtering what we are taught:

> *I pray this, that your love may abound even more and more in knowledge and every kind of insight so that you can decide what is best, and thus be sincere and blameless for the day of Christ, filled with the fruit of righteousness that comes through Jesus Christ to the glory and praise of God.* Philippians 1:9-11 NET

Now on to our first topic!

Chapter 3: Guaranteed Spouse?

Eduardo is a nice guy that I met at a party. He's a faithful Christian. God has used him in some extraordinary ways in the past. Eduardo has a strong prayer life and he can quote passage after passage of Scripture, rolling off of his tongue like honey.

A year ago Eduardo filed for divorce against his wife for repeated and unrepentant adultery. It was clearly a case which was biblically justified, as we'll see in the next chapter. Eduardo is convinced that God owes him a new wife. He reads the passages that he knows so well:

> *"And the LORD God said, It is not good that the man should be alone; I will make him a help meet for him."* (Genesis 2:18, in the King James Version which Eduardo memorizes.)

> *"Therefore shall a man leave his father and his mother, and shall cleave unto his wife: and they shall be one flesh."* (Genesis 2:24 KJV, also Matthew 19:5 and Ephesians 5:31)

> *"God setteth the solitary in families"* (Psalm 68:6 KJV)

> *"For the LORD hath called thee as a woman forsaken and grieved in spirit, and a wife of youth, when thou wast refused, saith thy God. For a small moment have I forsaken thee; but with great mercies will I gather thee. In a little wrath I hid my face from thee for a moment; but with everlasting kindness will I have mercy on thee, saith the LORD thy Redeemer."* (Isaiah 54:6-8 KJV)

> *"Thou shalt no more be termed Forsaken; neither shall thy land*

Guaranteed Spouse?

any more be termed Desolate: but thou shalt be called Hephzibah, and thy land Beulah: for the LORD delighteth in thee, and thy land shall be married." (Isaiah 62:4 KJV)

"If ye shall ask any thing in my name, I will do it." (John 14:14 KJV)

"And ye now therefore have sorrow: but I will see you again, and your heart shall rejoice, and your joy no man taketh from you. And in that day ye shall ask me nothing. Verily, verily, I say unto you, Whatsoever ye shall ask the Father in my name, he will give it you. Hitherto have ye asked nothing in my name: ask, and ye shall receive, that your joy may be full." (John 16:22-24 KJV)

"Nevertheless, to avoid fornication, let every man have his own wife, and let every woman have her own husband." (1st Corinthians 7:2 KJV)

"But my God shall supply all your need according to his riches in glory by Christ Jesus." (Philippians 4:19 KJV)

Eduardo has claimed these Scriptures as promises from God. And since he has asked for them in Jesus' name, he is sure that God will honor His promises. He believes God intends for every man to marry and has provided a special wife just for him.

Eduardo knows the Bible well. He has memorized huge portions of it. Unfortunately, he has allowed his need and desire to deceive him. These passages are taken quite out of context when used in this way; even a casual examination of most of them shows caveats immediately before or after them.

In short, God does not guarantee any person a spouse. There is nothing in the Bible that states this or even implies it. Most people will marry. But **there is no assurance from God that we will**.

If the circumstances of God's divine providence present themselves such that it is possible, by all means marry if you wish. We've already seen that is fine in God's plan. But don't let anyone trick you into believing that there is a guaranteed magical Mr. or Mrs. Right waiting out there. That is Hollywood talking, not the Bible.

Chapter 4: Divorce

In Appalachia, where I am from, they mine coal. My mother grew up in a town totally dominated by the mines and the railroads. Many modern mines use what used to be called "strip mining" and is now euphemistically called "mountaintop removal". Actually, maybe it's not a euphemism; that's a pretty accurate, if simplistic, description of exactly what they do. Picture a huge mountain. They literally cut off the entire top of the mountain and push all the rock into the holler or valley between it and the next mountain. Then they scoop out the coal, slap a little topsoil on what is left, scatter some grass seed, and move on to the next mountain.

If you have ever seen what is left afterwards, you will never forget it. The Appalachians are the most beautiful place on earth. And then you see a cut-off mountain. No matter what they tell you, no matter what they plant, the mountain will never be the same. It has been devastated, destroyed. The strong high rocks and wild vertical boundaries which define its existence, the very essence of its "mountain-ness", have been ripped

> Before we continue, I must caution you: If you are currently going through a divorce, put this book back on the shelf. It isn't for you. You will gain nothing from reading it and your money can be better spent on counseling – or at least on a good lawyer. Get godly advice from a wise pastor who knows your specific situation, not from a book which doesn't know anything about you. You can cherry-pick whatever you want, but you will not find godly wisdom or the answers you're looking for. Take it from me, divorce is going to be the most awful, painful, expensive thing that has ever happened to you.

away.

Divorce is like that. But then, you didn't need me to tell you that. You probably already know it first-hand. Divorce is the single most common shared characteristic of single people. Virtually every one of us has been affected by it. A quarter of us are divorced; many of the rest of us have divorced parents. A lot of us are paying the price today for the sins decades ago of our family members.

So you also understand why God hates divorce (Malachi 2:16). It is a ravenous monster that continues devouring lives long after the last papers are signed or the last check is written. But there is good news: whether the divorce was your own or you are dealing with the pain of parents who ripped your heart in half, you do not need to define yourself by your separateness any more than you have to define yourself by your singleness.

Get in a good divorce recovery class or class for the children of divorce; it will help you heal your broken heart. Divorce is a horrible sin, but it is not a scarlet letter. It is not the unforgivable sin. Which sin of yours – or of your parents' – did Christ not go to the cross for? Forgive others. Forgive yourself. Stop believing Satan's lie that it ruins you.

If you are divorced yourself, stop believing the Church's lie that it scars you forever, leaving you damaged goods. There are no second class citizens in the Kingdom of God. God loves you and died for you. Your debt has been paid. The blood of Jesus washes you whiter than snow.

This is not a treatise on the theology of divorce. However, so many of us face this issue that a brief look at it may be beneficial. The Bible is clear on the subject.

During the Sermon on the Mount, Jesus said, *"It was said, 'Whoever divorces his wife must give her a legal document.' But I say to you that everyone who divorces his wife, except for immorality, makes her commit adultery, and whoever marries a divorced woman commits adultery."* (Matthew 5:31-32 NET) Later, he repeated essentially the same thing to the Pharisees in Matthew 19. Paul reiterates it a third time, just repeating Jesus' teaching: *"To the married I give this command – not I, but the Lord – a wife should not divorce a husband (but if she does, let her remain unmarried, or be reconciled to her husband), and a husband should not divorce his wife."* (1st Corinthians 7:10-11 NET)

A problem arises, however, if we take from these passages the view frequently held by some churches. Many congregations hold that a Christian who divorces may never remarry, but of course a non-Christian's past sins are forgiven when they become a Christian. This is a reasonable theological view when applied with wisdom and a big dollop of mercy, but it is sometimes applied legalistically without common sense or compassion.

Someone can drag their spouse and children through a horrible divorce, then get saved, quickly meet and fall in love with another immature Christian, and get remarried, and it is fine with many churches, even though it is clear that they are headed for a repeat of the past. But a Christian who divorces at 20 or 30 and lives a deeply Christian life as a backbone of the Church for ten, twenty, or thirty years, may not get married when they meet another appropriate deeply godly person because this particular sin is not somehow forgivable.

This is not hypothetical. Both situations do occur, and more often than might be expected. As C.S. Lewis was fond of saying, "Our God is not a god of the absurd." An interpretation of Scripture that leads to nonsense or patent injustice must be suspect.

Jesus makes one exception above, for marital unfaithfulness. Paul, facing the practical questions of the early Church, lays out another exception for violence[4], *"But if the unbeliever wants a divorce, let it take place. In these circumstances the brother or sister is not bound. God has called you in peace."* (1st Corinthians 7:15 NET) He precedes this in v12 by saying that it wasn't the Lord's teaching, presumably because the exact topic never came up in Jesus' teachings, but that he is giving godly advice. The context of Paul's comments are the flash points where

---

4   1st Corinthians 7:15 has often been interpreted to mean that divorce is permitted when requested by an unbelieving spouse, and the second sentence in the verse has largely been ignored. An interpretation which better ties both parts of the verse together in context is that the determining factor is violence, and the assumption being that the violence shows that they are not Christian and they desire divorce. Regardless, in either case it is a single focused (though regrettably all too frequent) exception.

theology meets practical Christian living, and he mentions in v17 that he gives this advice (not just on divorce, but the other items covered in the chapter, as well) to all of the churches.

Humans were not meant to live alone. This is harsh teaching. Way harsh. The disciples give Jesus some rare push-back on this, *"The disciples said to him, 'If this is the case of a husband with a wife, it is better not to marry!'"* (Matthew 19:10 NET) They had the same problem with it that we do.

As we've already read, Jesus replied, *"Not everyone can accept this statement, except those to whom it has been given. For there are some eunuchs who were that way from birth, and some who were made eunuchs by others, and some who became eunuchs for the sake of the kingdom of heaven. The one who is able to accept this should accept it."* (Matthew 19:11-12 NET)

God's first and primary plan is for one man and one woman to be united for life. His fall-back position is that divorced people should not remarry. If you find yourself in this position, remaining unmarried is clearly God's direction - *"let her remain unmarried"* (1st Corinthians 7:11 NET). It can not be any plainer than that.

But Jesus recognized that not everyone could follow this teaching. So did Paul. He commands the married not to divorce. But if you are unmarried, here is what he says, *"To the unmarried and widows I say that it is best for them to remain as I am. But if they do not have self-control, let them get married. For it is better to marry than to burn with sexual desire."* (1st Corinthians 7:8-9 NET)

He did not say, "the virgins and widows". He said the "unmarried and widows". If you can remain unmarried, do so. But if it is consuming you inside, and if all other indications are positive, do not let a past mistake be the only thing that holds you back. That would be pride and a rejection of God's grace.

Do not take this for license. Indeed, you already know the price of divorce and do not need to be cautioned on it. But fully deal with the past before moving to the future. *"Submit to God. But resist the devil and he will flee from you. Draw near to God and he will draw near to*

Divorce

you. Cleanse your hands, you sinners, and make your hearts pure, you double-minded. Grieve, mourn, and weep. Turn your laughter into mourning and your joy into despair. Humble yourselves before the Lord and he will exalt you." (James 4:7-10 NET)

This is not God's ideal, but that was already shattered. And quite possibly through no fault of yours. *"Speak and act as those who will be judged by a law that gives freedom. For judgment is merciless for the one who has shown no mercy. But mercy triumphs over judgment."* (James 2:12-13 NET) Thank God that we serve a merciful God.

✔ See *Divorce and Remarriage: Four Christian Views*, by H. Wayne House for a good explanation of all major evangelical viewpoints on this topic.

Chapter 5: Dietrich Bonhoeffer

"This is the end... but for me the beginning of life."

Any study of the life of Dietrich Bonhoeffer must face the dichotomy of two men: one a professor who wrote the definitive book on Christian ethics; the other a member of a terrorist organization which put bombs in briefcases & on planes, and used suicide bombers with coats full of explosives, all in a vain attempt to assassinate the leader of his country.

One man was an early opponent of segregation for blacks in America; the other committed financial fraud to swindle his government out of thousands. The first was a pastor who traveled widely throughout Europe attempting to bring together Christians in the Ecumenical movement; the other traveled widely as an agent of military intelligence. One fled the country when the going got tough; the other marched resolutely through the gates of hell on earth and right up to the gallows. Both are Dietrich Bonhoeffer.

Dietrich and his twin sister Sabine were born on February 4, 1906 in Breslau, Germany. His family was upper-class and influential; his father was a leading psychiatrist. Dietrich was deeply affected by his brother's death during World War One and announced from an early age that he would become a clergyman.

When he was only 21, Dietrich received his doctorate in Theology from the University of Berlin. He also began a long-term stealth dating relationship[5] with Elizabeth Zinn, a fellow theologian. But after eight years, it ended badly, as most stealth dating does, and little more is known about it. Elizabeth undoubtedly played a major role in Dietrich's emotional life during his twenties, but she fades from the scene as does Orpah in the biblical book of Ruth.

Since he could not be ordained until 25, Dietrich spent the intervening time studying at the Union Theological Seminary in New York. During his stay in America, Dietrich worshiped frequently at the Abyssinian Baptist Church in black Harlem. He was profoundly disturbed by the segregation around him.

In 1931 the storm clouds were gathering in Germany and Dietrich returned home, bringing with him a large collection of African American spirituals and jazz records. Dietrich understood and opposed the Nazi threat from the very beginning because his twin sister had married a Jew.

This did not make him popular with his Lutheran church because most evangelical Christians supported the Nazis as a counterbalance to atheistic communism. The Nazis played a finely tuned game of encouraging the Christians to think of Adolf Hitler as a supporter and proponent of Christianity and the state church, while at the same time ever increasing their financial and political control over the church.

Dietrich fought them every step of the way. He became a leader of the international ecumenical movement and reached out to his English and European brothers and sisters to partner in stemming the growing flood of Nazi hatred. Later during the war years, the friendships that he made during this period would be instrumental. Nevertheless, the Nazis were successful not only in coming to power (in large part thanks to the protestant Christian vote), but in actually seizing control of the state church. They banned Dietrich from speaking and he went abroad to briefly pastor German-speaking churches in England and Spain.

Martin Niemoller, Karl Barth, and other leaders formed the Confessing

---

5   Stealth Dating is when neither party acknowledges their relationship as anything but friendship, but it is far more. Stealth dating can last for years and lead to spiritual and emotional fornication as the lovers live life as a couple in every sense except physical consummation and the sacrament of marriage. When it ends, it can often be nearly as painful as divorce.

Dietrich Bonhoeffer

Church to stand in opposition to the Nazi-controlled Lutheran Church. They asked Dietrich to return to Germany and lead an illegal underground seminary for the training of pastors.

The Nazis kept squeezing restrictions around Dietrich and the Confessing Church tighter and tighter. He was not allowed to preach, then forbidden to teach, and finally to speak publicly in any way. They arrested leader after leader of the Confessing Church, sending each in turn to the concentration camps, until finally there were no dynamic leaders left and the Church lost heart and withered. Like many of his contemporaries, Dietrich fled Germany for America; he was offered a teaching position where he could sit out the coming war in safety.

Dietrich suffered from severe depression throughout his life. When he arrived in America, he spent weeks lying in bed. Finally he decided,

> I have made a mistake in coming to America. I shall have no right to participate in the reconstruction of the Christian life in Germany after the war if I did not share in the trials of this time with my people. Christians in Germany will face the terrible alternative of either willing the defeat of their nation in order that Christian civilization may survive, or willing the victory of their nation and thereby destroying our civilization. I know which of these alternatives I must choose, but I cannot make that choice in security.

He returned to Germany on the very eve of war. When Germany invaded Poland in September, 1939, Dietrich was due to be called up with virtually all other German men of military age. As a long time pacifist, the thought of serving the Nazi war machine was abhorrent to him. His friends helped him become an agent of the Abwehr, German military intelligence, an organization rife with opponents to Hitler. Dietrich was supposed to travel Europe using his contacts with the protestant churches in other countries to aid the German war effort. In reality his trips abroad were the perfect cover for his two new true activities.

By this time Dietrich had joined several of his family members in the plot to assassinate Adolf Hitler. Dietrich's pacifism abhorred all manner of violence, but as the Nazi atrocities deepened, he came to the

Dietrich Bonhoeffer

conclusion, "Anyone who is not ready to kill Hitler is guilty of mass murder, whether he likes it or not." He served as a go-between coordinating their activities with the British intelligence services and providing moral and ethical support.

Dietrich was also using his new found power as an agent of the Abwehr to hide German Jews and then later smuggle them out of the country to Switzerland. He embezzled German government funds to pay for these activities.

While Dietrich was active in the underground, his personal life also underwent a profound change. On January 17, 1943, at age 36, he became engaged to be married to 18-year-old Maria von Wedemeyer. Her grandmother was Dietrich's long time friend and principle financial supporter, Dutchess Ruth von Kleist-Retzow. Maria's family was skeptical because of the age difference[6], but Maria proved a faithful rock during the trying time to come.

The Resistance made a variety of attempts to kill Hitler; something always went wrong. Several times suicide volunteers carrying explosives in their overcoats attempted to embrace Hitler and blow themselves up, but he always had a last minute change of schedule. A bomb was placed on his plane, but it failed to explode.

The Gestapo could not come up with enough evidence to arrest Dietrich or the others because of their influential friends. But eventually, the Gestapo discovered Dietrich's embezzlement and how it linked to the escaping Jews. In March 1943, they arrested him and his brother-in-law, throwing them in prison.

Maria visited the succession of prisons in which Dietrich was held, though she was rarely allowed to see him. She marked out in chalk a rectangle the size of his cell on her bedroom floor so that as they exchanged letters she could write to him as if they were together. After the war, their correspondence would be published as *Love Letters from*

---

6 Dietrich clearly had never heard of the Creepiness Algorithm, $D >= (A / 2) + 7$. Never ask anyone out who is younger than your age divided by two and plus 7. The Creepiness Algorithm works for a wide variety of ages: 20 (17), 30 (22), 40 (27), 50 (32). Nevertheless, Dietrich and Maria are perhaps the exception that proves the rule.

Dietrich Bonhoeffer

Cell 92.

For the remainder of the war, the Gestapo interrogated Dietrich and attempted to get evidence to burst open the conspiracy. He never gave in. On June 20, 1944, after Dietrich had been in prison for over a year, the plotters exploded a suitcase bomb in Hitler's bunker and launched a simultaneous coup attempt in Berlin and Paris. Incredibly, although the room was destroyed, four people were killed, and five seriously injured, Hitler survived with only minor injuries. Troops loyal to him quickly quashed the coup.

Hitler's revenge was swift and terrible. Five thousand people were arrested. All of the blood relatives of the plotters were thrown in prison. About two hundred people were gruesomely strangled to death slowly, including many unconnected to the plot. Dietrich's brother Klaus and brothers-in-law, Hans von Dohnanyi and Rudiger Schleicher, fellow plot members, were executed.

Dietrich's innocence in the specific June 20th attempt was manifest by virtue of his being in prison, but the Gestapo were sure of his involvement in the broader plot. On April 9, 1945, just days before the Flossenburg concentration camp was liberated by advancing Russian forces, the executioners came for Dietrich and six other remaining opponents of Hitler. He entrusted a book to a British POW inscribed with a last message for his friend, Bishop George Bell, "This is the end... but for me the beginning of life." The Nazi SS doctor who attended his hanging said afterwards, "I have never seen a man die so completely submissive to the will of God."

✔ There is an embarrassment of riches if you would like to find out more about Dietrich Bonhoeffer. He wrote a number of books on theology; they are translated from German and are not for the faint of heart. The best known are *Ethics*, *The Cost of Discipleship*, and *Letters & Papers from Prison*. *Life Together* is an easier read, about living in authentic Christian community. All these are available in a variety of editions & publishers. *Love Letters From Cell 92* is out of print.

Dietrich Bonhoeffer

There are a number of biographies of Dietrich's life. *Dietrich Bonhoeffer: a Biography*, by his friend and protege, Eberhard Bethge, who lived through many of the events of the conspiracy with Dietrich, is considered the classic. *Till the Night Be Past: The Life and Times of Dietrich Bonhoeffer*, by Theodore Kleinhans, is a perhaps more approachable recent effort. Two biographical movies have also been made, *Bonhoeffer*, and *Hanging on a Twisted Cross: The Life, Convictions, and Martyrdom of Dietrich Bonhoeffer*. They are based on nearly identical archival materials and the first is the more interesting of the two.

Historical fiction is the most enjoyable way to learn about Dietrich. The movie, *Bonhoeffer: Agent of Grace*, is meticulously accurate and quite interesting; it makes a great small group evening. The book, *Saints and Villains*, by Denise Giardina takes a few more liberties but is also an excellent story.

Chapter 6: Depression

✝ I'm so depressed that nobody will love me.

How do you read that sentence? (Go back and read it again.) Which came first, the chicken or the egg? Depression is the second largest common characteristic (after divorce) for older singles. But are we unmarried because we are depressed? Or are we depressed because we are unmarried?

The truth is that depression can be a vicious circle for unmarried people that feeds upon itself like a snake eating its own tail. Some of us are unmarried as a symptom of the fact that we are depressed or emotionally unhealthy for other psychological reasons. Some of us are depressed because of the circumstances of our singleness. And many of us have been around this vicious circle so often that there's no telling which is the case.

We're not alone. Amy Carmichael's depression was a large part of what forced her off of the mission field during her first term of service in Japan. In later years, she exhibited some behavior that today we might call bipolar. Dietrich Bonhoeffer struggled with "can't get out of bed" level serious depression his entire life. Despite this, both of them achieved great things for God.

And so can we. Depression is better understood and much more treatable than it was just a few years ago. Often depression is an issue directly related to the physical chemistry of the brain. Other times, depression is caused by our circumstances. After all, everyone gets

Depression

down when they have a good reason to be sad; that's normal and healthy.

Depression breeds depression. It also provides a fertile breeding ground for sin. The times when we feel the most down are the times that we are the most vulnerable to the sins that bedevil us. "All is hopeless, so why not? I feel bad and it feels good. At least I will feel <u>something</u> for a little while."

But it's a trap. Afterwards the guilt will come and drive us even lower, worthless worms that we are. After all, all that grace stuff is for everyone but us. If nobody else loves us (& like many lies of Satan, this one may start with a grain of truth – or not, after all, he is the father of lies), then why should God love us either?

Is this the life God wants us to live? Let's go to the Bible and see what Jesus has to say on the topic: *"I have come so that they may have life, and may have it abundantly."* (John 10:10 NET) The NET Bible's translator's notes says, "That is, more than one would normally expect or anticipate." Does that describe your single life? Do you have life more than your friends would anticipate? Or are you sitting at home moping?

God doesn't want us to be lonely or alone. Jesus may have been single, but he was a party animal. Jesus said of himself, *"The Son of Man has come eating and drinking, and you say, 'Look at him, a glutton and a drunk, a friend of tax collectors and sinners!'"* (Luke 7:74 NET) He surrounded himself with friends and was well known for partying with drinkers.

For some of us, this comes naturally to our sanguine nature. But for the rest of us melancholy phlegmatics, we may have to work at it. The nice thing about singleness is that we are free to do what we want when we want. We can be spontaneous because we don't have to check what our spouse has planned for the weekend. That's cool and that's one of the advantages we can enjoy in our situation. But don't let that keep you from filling your schedule.

If you know that you get depressed when you sit at home, get out. Plan your evenings. Let's see: Sunday evening church, Tuesday evening small group, Wednesday evening leadership meeting (you are serving somehow, right?), Friday night Guys' Night, Saturday dinner with

Depression

friends. That's easy and still leaves Monday and Thursday evenings to do laundry and crash. It isn't any more healthy to fill every waking moment with friends than it is to exclude them. Jesus had plenty of alone time as well as party time.

Keep active. Any number of times I have had to drag myself to go out with my friends or to a Bible study, yet afterwards I am always glad that I did. It's kind of like exercise: I hate starting it, but afterwards my body feels good. Our social life requires exercise just like our physical bodies do. And one powerful counter for depression is simply being around other people.

Learn to avoid "downers" and use "uppers". Watch yourself and learn the things that bring you down. Avoid them. Some common ones:

- Getting too tired.
- Sleeping too much. (Yes, sleeping too much can actually make you feel more tired.)
- Getting hungry. Or pigging out.
- Darkness. For me there is no bigger downer than coming home to a dark quiet house. I ignore the electric bill and leave a florescent light on in the kitchen to greet me.

Learn the things that bring you up in healthy ways and maximize your exposure to them. Some common ones:

- Music
- The outdoors. Learn the area hiking trails! Look up and see the stars at night.
- Exercise. You don't have to start with a marathon. Just get out and walk around the block every single day for two weeks. You'll be amazed how much better you feel afterwards than before!
- Sunshine. Open the curtains!

Lastly, don't be afraid to get professional help. A lot of people do. As mentioned, we now know a lot more about how the brain works chemically and a professional can often really help.

Depression

But use wisdom; for every good psychiatrist, psychologist, or counselor out there, there is an ineffective one. It may take you a couple of tries to find a good one. But on the other hand, if you go through a number of them without finding any that you like, consider that it may be you and not them. You will get out of counseling exactly what you put into it.

How can you tell if you need professional help? If your depression is impacting your ability to function as a productive member of society and your church, then get help. What are the alternatives? Either they help you overcome your depression and all is well, or they don't and at least you're no worse off than you were before.

✔ There are many good resources for helping yourself deal with depression. There is also some bad advice, so use discernment. A counselor or pastor can point you towards good ones. A great place to start is

http://www.helpguide.org/mental/depression_tips.htm

which has concrete practical tips, as well as links to other resources.

Chapter 7: Betsie and Corrie ten Boom

"[We] must tell them what we have learned here. We must tell them that there is no pit so deep that He is not deeper still. They will listen to us, Corrie, because we have been here."

Betsie ten Boom was born on August 19, 1885, the first of five children for Caspar and Cornelia ten Boom, of Haarlem, in Holland (the Netherlands). Her sister Corrie was born seven years later on April 15, 1892, premature and the fifth and last of the ten Boom children.

The ten Boom family lived in the Beje, an ancient three-floor row house made from two separate abutting buildings which had been joined together. The 100 year old family watch shop was on the ground floor. The ten Booms were a deeply Christian family.

The Beje was a merry house full of people. In addition to Caspar, Cornelia, and their five children, they also had three older aunts who lived with them. In later years as the aunts passed away and their siblings married and moved out, they kept many foster children. There was always room in the Beje for one more.

In 1918, Betsie and Corrie's mother, Cornelia, suffered a cerebral hemorrhage and became unable to speak; three years later she passed away. But this didn't change the nature of the Beje. They continued to take in and raise needy children, as well as extend hospitality to anyone passing through.

Betsie was diagnosed early in her life with juvenile pernicious anemia.

Betsie and Corrie ten Boom

It was clear that physically she could never have children. Betsie made a conscious decision never to marry.

When Corrie was twenty-three, she was deeply hurt by a man who courted her for several years. Her family saw that he was unlikely to follow through because his parents planned an upper-class marriage and he was too weak to refuse, but Corrie would not listen to them. When he turned up one day with his wealthy new fiancé, Corrie was devastated.

As the years passed, the ten Booms settled into a long-term domestic pattern. Betsie kept the books for the watch shop, Corrie tended to the house, and their father made and repaired watches. When Betsie grew ill one winter, she was forced to move away from the shop door and take over the domestics, leaving Corrie to tend the store.

They both discovered that they loved their new roles much better than the last. Betsie was a better housekeeper, while Corrie was a natural in the watch shop. After setting the chaotic books straight, she soon began training as a watchmaker. In 1922, Corrie became the Netherlands' first female licensed watchmaker.

Corrie also spent the 1920s and 1930s organizing girls' clubs and programs for the handicapped and developmentally disabled. These clubs grew quite large and occupied much of her free evening time.

Betsie and Corrie's brother Willem went to seminary and became a pastor. His graduate dissertation in 1927 was on the dangers of Germanic antisemitism. Few took it – or him – seriously. But the storm clouds rolled in. For the first time in their shop's one-hundred year history, Caspar had to fire a young German journeyman watchmaker who abused another elderly employee; later during the war he would turn out to be a German officer who had been exploring Holland.

On May 10, 1940, Germany invaded the Netherlands. Betsie was 54. Corrie was 48. Until the war, Betsie and Corrie had lived quiet Christian lives. Neither was a public speaker. Neither had written a book. Neither woman had done anything to bring them to anyone's attention.

The Nazis quickly banned Corrie's girls clubs, but not because they were threatened by them. Rather, they banned all public gatherings. They

Betsie and Corrie ten Boom

simply took no serious notice of the ten Boom family.

The ten Boom family took notice of the Nazis, though. As committed Christians in the Calvinist heritage, they had a deep respect for the Jews as God's chosen people. It quickly became known throughout Haarlem that a Jew could always expect a meal and a kind word at the Beje.

For two years, the ten Booms gradually drifted into more and more active roles in protection of their neighborhood Jews. Willem, who lived outside of town and pastored a small rural church, was the first to cross the line into the organized underground. The local rabbi and others brought their Torahs and other religious items to the Beje for safekeeping.

One night the Beje received a frightened visitor, Mrs. Kleermaker. Her husband had been arrested by the Gestapo and their shop closed down. Now she was afraid to return to their tiny apartment for fear that she too would be arrested.

"In this household," Caspar told her, "God's people are always welcome." That started a steady stream of Jewish refugees who sought their protection. At first, they would house them for a short time while Willem found them long-term places to stay in the countryside. Eventually it became difficult to find safe housing and their stays became longer.

Over the next two years, the ten Booms became the hub of the Haarlem underground. Because Caspar was in his eighties and growing increasingly feeble and absent-minded, it was really Betsie and Corrie who did all of the work. Betsie was responsible for keeping them fed and cared for, while Corrie was responsible for keeping them safe, finding homes for them, and keeping them supplied.

The underground sent a "Mr. Smith" who built them a secret room for Jews to hide in during danger. Mr. Smith was actually one of the Netherland's foremost architects and the Beje's hiding place was a masterpiece. The new construction blended exactly into the old building's stained walls. They averaged 6-7 people a night hiding there for two years.

Finally, on February 28, 1944, the ten Booms were betrayed and the

Betsie and Corrie ten Boom

Gestapo raided the Beje. It was a massive raid and caught not only the ten Booms, but many others of their underground cell. The Germans strongly suspected that there were Jews hiding in the house, but they could not find them. They knocked holes in the walls and left a guard, but the hiding place went undiscovered. Several days later the underground was able to get the Jews to safety. All but one survived the war.

Caspar was 84 and frail in both body and mind when they were arrested. The chief of the Gestapo told him, "I'd like to send you home, old fellow. I'll take your word that you won't cause any more trouble."

He replied strongly and clearly, "If I go home today, tomorrow I will open my door again to any man in need who knocks." He was separated from the others and sent to what passed as a hospital. Ten days later he was dead, left in a cold corridor with no care.

Betsie, Corrie, and Willem were all sent to prison at Scheveningen, near the Hague. Willem was soon released; two years later he would die of the tuberculosis he contracted in prison. During their time at Scheveningen, the women were separated, but each received smuggled Scriptures.

On June 6, 1944 the Allies invaded France and everyone's hopes rose for a quick end to the war. It didn't happen, and Betsie and Corrie were moved to a labor camp at Vught, Holland.

The war continued to go badly for Germany, and in September of that year the ten Booms were moved to Ravensbruck concentration camp in Germany. Through a long string of coincidences, their Bible was missed every time they were searched.

At Ravensbruck, Betsie and Corrie began holding forbidden prayer services for the prisoners. Betsie became the rock which held everyone together. While Corrie despaired over their living conditions, Betsie thanked God for the lice. Later they would come to realize that the guards left the prisoners alone when they were in their barracks because the buildings were infested with lice.

Ravensbruck took its inevitable toll on the ten Booms, though. On December 16, 1944, Betsie died. Her last words were, "[we] must tell them what we have learned here. We must tell them that there is no pit so deep that He is not deeper still. They will listen to us, Corrie, because we have been here."

Two weeks later, on December 31, Corrie was unexpectedly released from Ravensbruck due to a clerical error. A week later all the women in the ten Booms' block were sent to the gas chamber.

Corrie made her way back to Haarlem and discovered that Willem's son had died in a German POW camp. She immediately threw herself into trying to help other similar victims of the Nazis. As she started her work, the war ground to an agonizing end. On May 5, 1945, Holland was liberated, and then three days later Germany surrendered.

All of Europe was in shambles. Sixty million people were dead. Millions more were maimed. Tens of millions of victims were psychologically traumatized by the Germans. Germany herself was devastated; most German men were dead or prisoners of war and 90% of all the women in eastern Germany were raped. Tens of thousands of collaborators and German war criminals were still loose and trying to rebuild their lives right alongside their victims.

Less than a month after the end of the war, a wealthy woman donated a large house, Schapenduinen in Bloemendaal, Holland, to Corrie for her rehabilitation work. Corrie worked first with traumatized victims.

As time went on, it became clear that the major issue victims were dealing with was reconciliation with their oppressors. It also became clear that many of the perpetrators were having serious problems with guilt.

A year later, in 1946, the Germans offered Corrie the Darmstadt concentration camp. It reopened as a rehabilitation home. Corrie's work expanded into helping victims forgive and Germans repent and accept forgiveness.

Corrie was 53 when the war ended. She spent the rest of her life in a worldwide ministry of forgiveness. In 1968 she was declared a Righteous Gentile by Israel for saving Jews during the war. For over thirty-five years, wherever there were shattered lives left in the aftermath of conflict, she helped people learn to forgive.

Betsie and Corrie ten Boom

She said of her own suffering,

> Looking back across the years of my life, I can see the working of a divine pattern which is the way of God with His children. When I was in a prison camp in Holland during the war, I often prayed, 'Lord, never let the enemy put me in a German concentration camp.' God answered no to that prayer. Yet in the German camp, with all its horror, I found many prisoners who had never heard of Jesus Christ.
>
> If God had not used my sister Betsie and me to bring them to Him, they would never have heard of Him. Many died, or were killed, but many died with the name of Jesus on their lips. They were well worth all our suffering. Faith is like radar which sees through the fog—the reality of things at a distance that the human eye cannot see.

Corrie died on April 15, 1983, her 91st birthday.

✔ To find out more about Betsie and Corrie ten Boom, read *The Hiding Place*, by Corrie ten Boom, or watch the movie of the same name.

Chapter 8: Hatred and Hurt

- Her earliest memory is of her father beating her mother and thinking, "When I grow up, I'm going to kill him."

- They hadn't been able to keep their hands off each other before marriage, but six months after the wedding, the lust wore off. She rolled over one morning and calmly announced, "I hate you." Over the coming years she showed it was a simple statement of fact as she turned his life into hell in a dozen different ways.

- The social worker found the four-year-old covered in flour and eggs, sitting on the floor crying. Cans of soup and bottles of beer had bruised him. The police had taken his mother away screaming after neighbors reported her. She had thrown the contents of two bags of groceries at him as he cowered in the corner.

- Jack's aunt explained that his mother was sick with cancer. He understood, in a nine-year-old sort of way. His Sunday School teacher told him that God answers prayers if you really believe. Jack did, and so he prayed, fully expecting God to heal his mother. God answered – or so he thought – and she got better for a brief time. But then she quickly sickened further and died.

There are so many examples that we could go on and on... We have been hurt so badly it boggles the mind. Atrocities have been committed. Our parents or our spouses or our boyfriend or

Hatred and Hurt

girlfriend have destroyed us. Or maybe a step-parent or relative. Or boss. Or a backstabbing "friend". Or maybe it is just circumstance or a string of incredibly bad luck.

Or maybe it was God who hurt us. He's supposed to be in charge, right? If he loved us like he says, how could it have happened?

Words really are inadequate to describe the situation. The best argument for atheism or deism[7] is the condition of this planet on which we find ourselves. It isn't just hurting or "fallen". It is truly screwed up beyond any human measure. The amount of suffering in the world is hardly imaginable.

A number of great Christians have struggled with this issue. Among them are one whose story we have already read and one who we will read about in a coming chapter. Both are uniquely qualified to address the topic.

C.S. Lewis's *The Problem of Pain* addresses the question from a theological standpoint. The book is great reading and deals with all of the intellectual problems wrapped up in unjust suffering. At its heart, C.S. Lewis believed that pain is unavoidable in a world where God has given us free will. However, God has sent His son as a fellow sufferer in order to bring justice as well as salvation.

(With a better understanding of the nature of time and eternity, some Christians now believe that both sides of the old debate over free will versus predestination are correct, depending upon your point of view. Free will and predestination exist in a paradox. This makes C.S. Lewis's explanation of the problem compatible with both great Protestant heritages.)

Once as I was praying, my heart cried out to God over Africa, "God, how long are you going to allow all of the ethnic violence, corruption, illness, and starvation of Africa to continue? How long are people groups who want your Gospel going to have to continue in darkness because the Scriptures do not exist in their language? How long will the African witch-doctors keep their people living in fear and bondage?"

---

7   Deism is the belief that God the creator of the universe may exist somewhere out there, but isn't interested in our personal lives.

Hatred and Hurt

A short time later I was reading the history of African missions in the 1800s. Hundreds of nineteenth-century Christian missionaries went to Africa. They shipped their belongings in a casket, because they anticipated being sent home in it. Most came, stayed a few months or years, became ill, and died. Africa was truly the White Man's Graveyard.

"God, wouldn't it have been a wiser use of your resources for those missionaries to have evangelized Asia? Or at least Europe or North America where they could have a more effective ministry instead of wasting their lives. Then in the twentieth century when modern medicine made it less dangerous[8], the Church could have focused on Africa."

But he reminded me of my previous prayer and of the parable of the tenants:

> *"Listen to another parable: There was a landowner who planted a vineyard. He put a fence around it, dug a pit for its winepress, and built a watchtower. Then he leased it to tenant farmers and went on a journey. When the harvest time was near, he sent his slaves to the tenants to collect his portion of the crop. But the tenants seized his slaves, beat one, killed another, and stoned another. Again he sent other slaves, more than the first, and they treated them the same way. Finally he sent his son to them, saying, 'They will respect my son.' But when the tenants saw the son, they said to themselves, 'This is the heir. Come, let's kill him and get his inheritance!' So they seized him, threw him out of the vineyard, and killed him."* (Matthew 21:33-39 NET; cf Luke 20:9-15)

Even though missionaries died like flies, God never stopped loving the people of Africa and sent them a continuous stream of missionaries, not only in the 1800s, but continuing in the 1900s and even today. He saw the suffering of the African people and sent his servants to bring them the Good News, along with mission schools and hospitals. He loved enough to send the very best, including His only Son. What more could

---

8   This was before I had actually suffered through all the modern medicine necessary to survive in Africa...

Hatred and Hurt

He have done?

If C.S. Lewis explores the intellectual aspect of why God allows pain and suffering, Corrie ten Boom comes at it from another angle altogether. As she lived, God gradually taught her how to forgive. Remembering when she was 23 and the man she loved married another, she wrote,

> How long I lay on my bed sobbing for the one love of my life I do not know. Later, I heard Father's footsteps coming up the stairs. For a moment I was a little girl again waiting for him to tuck the blankets tight. But this was a hurt that no blanket could shut out, and suddenly I was afraid of what Father would say. Afraid he would say, "There'll be someone else soon," and that forever afterward this untruth would lie between us. For in some deep part of me I knew already that there would not – soon or ever – be anyone else.
>
> The sweet cigar-smell came into the room with Father. And of course he did not say the false, idle words.
>
> "Corrie," he began instead, "do you know what hurts so very much? It's love. Love is the strongest force in the world, and when it is blocked that means pain.
>
> "There are two things we can do when this happens. We can kill the love so that it stops hurting. But then of course part of us dies, too. Or, Corrie, we can ask God to open up another route for that love to travel.
>
> "God loves Karel – even more than you do – and if you ask Him, He will give you His love for this man, a love nothing can prevent, nothing destroy. Whenever we cannot love in the old, human way, Corrie, God can give us the perfect way."
>
> I did not know, as I listened to Father's footsteps winding back down the stairs, that he had given me more than the key to this hard moment. I did not know that he had put into my hands the secret that would open far darker rooms than this – places where there was not, on a human level, anything to love at all.
>
> I was still in kindergarten in these matters of love. My task just

Hatred and Hurt

then was to give up my feeling for Karel without giving up the joy and wonder that had grown with it. And so, that very hour, lying there on my bed, I whispered the enormous prayer:

"Lord, I give to You the way I feel about Karel, my thoughts about our future – oh, You know! Everything! Give me Your way of seeing Karel instead. Help me to love him that way. That much."

And even as I said the words I fell asleep. (*The Hiding Place*, Corrie ten Boom, pp64-65)

Weddings are often such a bittersweet event for us. Aunts or grandmothers hassle us with snide remarks like, "Isn't it about time to settle down?" or "I guess I'm never going to get grandchildren..." Maybe no one says anything, but how can it be possible to be so joyful for our friends and yet so aching for ourselves at the same time? Our families and friends enjoy be the blessings for which we long. Four years later, Corrie was at her sister Nollie's wedding when she finally realized that she would never marry,

> Now I was twenty-seven, Betsie in her mid-thirties, and I knew that this was the way it was going to be: Betsie and I the unmarried daughters living at home in the Beje.
>
> It was a happy thought, not a sad one. And that was the moment when I knew for sure that God had accepted the faltering gift of my emotions made four years ago. For with the thought of Karel – all shining round with love as thoughts of him had been since I was fourteen – came not the slightest trace of hurt. "Bless Karel, Lord Jesus," I murmured under my breath. "And bless her. Keep them close to one another and to You." And that was a prayer, I knew for sure, that could not have sprung unaided from Corrie ten Boom. (*The Hiding Place*, Corrie ten Boom, p69)

Corrie forgave Karel in her head the very night of his betrayal, but it took four years for it to filter into her heart and to honestly wish him and his wife happiness. God teaches forgiveness slowly through life.

As horrible as someone dumping us is, God knew that she would have to forgive far worse in the future. A few weeks after the end of the war,

Hatred and Hurt

Corrie was told the identity of the man who betrayed her family to the Gestapo. She wrote him a letter:

> Dear Sir:
>
> Today I heard that most probably you were the one who betrayed me. I went through ten months of concentration camp. My father died after 10 days, my sister after ten months of imprisonment.
>
> What you meant to be harmful, God used for my good. I have become closer to Him. A severe punishment is awaiting you. I have prayed for you that the Lord will accept you if you will turn to Him. Think about the fact that the Lord Jesus also carried your sins on the cross. If you accept that and will be His child, you will be saved forever.
>
> I have forgiven you everything; God will forgive you everything also, if you ask Him. He loves you, and He, Himself has sent His son to earth to forgive you your sins, that is, to bear the punishment for you and me. From your side an answer must be given. When He says "Come to me, give your heart," then your answer must be: "Yes, Lord, I will. Make me your child."
>
> If you have difficulty praying, ask then if God will give you his Spirit; He works the faith in your heart. Never doubt the love of the Lord Jesus. He stands with His arms wide open to receive you.
>
> I hope that the hard road that you now have to go will bring you to your eternal Savior. (http://www.theeffectivechristian.org/new Chapter 9, Corrie ten Boom.htm)

Before she wrote the letter, she felt the same hatred and anger in her heart that we feel for those who have hurt us, even for God himself. In her own strength she could not have forgiven the man responsible for all her family's pain. But with the help of the Holy Spirit, Corrie was able to forgive from the heart.

God is love. God is omnipotent. The world hurts so badly that God took extraordinary steps to fix it. He has done everything necessary to redeem it. He sent his only son, the one he loved, to suffer to save each and every hurting wounded soul. The work of redemption is ongoing in the sense that we must accept this wonderful gift and also in the sense that, until he returns, this world is enemy territory. The war is as surely won as World War II was once the D-Day landings were a success. But here, as then, there will be "plenty of hell behind, and plenty of hell ahead" before it is over.

It sounds like such a cop out to say that bad people get their just desserts in the end, but that doesn't prevent it from being true. Jesus' parable concludes, *"Now when the owner of the vineyard comes, what will he do to those tenants?" They said to him, "He will utterly destroy those evil men! Then he will lease the vineyard to other tenants who will give him his portion at the harvest."* (Matthew 21:40-41 NET)

Many churches now have workshops that can help you overcome hurt and forgive those responsible. Don't be afraid to reach out for wisdom and strength from others.

✔ C.S. Lewis's *The Problem of Pain* is a great book to read dealing with this issue. Corrie ten Boom also wrote extensively on the topic, but except for *The Hiding Place*, most of her books are out of print.

Chapter 9: Meddling (Theirs)

> ✝ "We meddle... People don't like to be meddled with. We tell them what to do, what to think, don't run, don't walk. We're in their homes and in their heads, and we haven't the right. We're meddlesome." River Tam, *Serenity*

I shared the breakfast table at an African guest house with an older missionary couple from another organization. I'd never met them before. The wife quickly started the conversation rolling, "Tell me about your wife and children."

"I'm not married. Pass the milk, please."

A few moments while she thought on this. "Why aren't you married yet?" she demanded next.

My first thought, which I had to consciously choke off, was, "Why aren't you divorced yet?" Did she really want me to get into my entire life story at the breakfast table with complete strangers? I turned the other cheek and muttered something about "I'm just serving the Lord."

My next couple of minutes were spent on thoughts of caffeine and waking up, but she clearly was chewing on my answer. After a bit, she burst into a loud soliloquy, "I just can't understand people that don't want children. My three have been such a blessing to me on the mission field and allowed me to be so effective..." On she rambled for a while about the blessings of marriage.

Yes, lady. So you've had to raise three or four times the support that I have, and spent a large part of your time taking care of them. You've

Meddling (Theirs)

already stuck a dagger into my gut, and now you're stabbing one through my heart.

Don't you think I would give everything in a heartbeat for a family? Don't you think I've spent countless hours praying for them? God hasn't seen fit to give me that blessing, but he certainly has allowed me other things in my present lifestyle to make up for it.

I kept my head down and said nothing else at breakfast, so hurt that I just wanted to get out of there as quickly as possible.

Haven't we all been in a similar situation? Or our aunt or our hairdresser tries to fix us up with someone we've never met, and in honesty they barely even know themselves.

When people say things like this to us, they are committing the sin of meddling, especially if they aren't close to us.

The Thessalonian church had a problem with meddling, and Paul wrote to them, *"to aspire to lead a quiet life, to attend to your own business, and to work with your hands, as we commanded you."* 1 Thessalonians 4:11 NET

They must not have listened, because later he wrote again, *"For we hear that some among you are living an undisciplined life, not doing their own work but meddling in the work of others. Now such people we command and urge in the Lord Jesus Christ to work quietly and so provide their own food to eat."* 2 Thessalonians 3:11-12

What are we to do in response to such hurtful sin? Jesus says to turn the other cheek (Matthew 5:39 & Luke 6:29). What does that mean when confronted with this type of sin?

It doesn't mean dealing with it the way that I did. By ignoring her initial meddling and sinful question, and burying my hurt, I set both of us up for further sin. First of all, she continued to meddle, and dove into my singleness in an even more hurtful way than she had before.

And I may have drawn the walls up around my shocked hurt, but you better believe that it affected my interaction with her in the future. Later, I was invited to eat lunch with a whole table of people. I turned it down flat simply because I didn't want to sit near her. By not

Meddling (Theirs)

confronting her sin head-on, I let it poison my entire relationship with her.

We should not ignore the rude questions, statements, or actions of those who denigrate our singleness. On the other hand, it is dangerous to confront someone even in a loving way, especially if we don't know them very well.

Perhaps the simplest approach is best. Most people saying these hurtful things are not aware that they are being rude or hurtful. Simply and politely tell them so, "That was a rude thing to say. It hurt my feelings." The phrase, "None of your business.", politely said, is <u>not</u> rude. If they choose to take offense at polite correction, that's their issue, not ours.

What about when those who are closer to us do the same thing? The dreaded, "Oh, I guess I'll just never be a grandmother..." isn't so easily handled. We love these people enough that they can hurt us deeply. Worse, yet, sometimes they know very well that what they are saying is hurtful.

It's a lot more difficult, but the same course is appropriate. We identify the behavior as rude and hurtful. We ask them not to continue. If they do, we let them know that we're leaving because we won't be a part of an unhealthy conversation, then we do so.

This assumes that we have our own home to go to. As an adult, we should be living our own lives. Even if we're honoring our father or mother by taking care of them in illness or old age, if it is for an extended period of time, then we should be doing so from our own home. We should have our own house or apartment, perhaps with a roommate, but not living at home. Otherwise, we're inviting being treated as a child.

What do we do when it's our friends giving us dating advice or playing matchmaker? When friends or close nuclear family do that, we probably should pay attention. They do know us, and they have our best interests at heart.

That doesn't mean we should necessarily take their advice, but at least consider it carefully. They can often see something we can't about a person. Generally, their advice is sometimes wise when it is negative,

Meddling (Theirs)

but it's usually spot-on when it is positive. They love us and want only good things for us.

If we don't want any matchmaking, even from those close to us, simply tell them so, and then expect them to respect our decision. If we are open (or desperate!), then let them know in a friendly way. It's a mark of trust and profound respect for their judgment. Just don't expect miracles from them!

Before we move on, there's one more way in which people meddle in our lives as singles. It's sad to say, but often churches and other religious organizations treat singles in ways they don't treat married people.

Let's realize right up front that 1st Corinthians 7:32-36 is clear. We have chosen (or, at least, are stuck in) a more desirable path. We have nothing to apologize for. There is <u>nothing</u> in Scripture to support any idea that singles are lesser persons. And church history, contrary to what many married pastors may believe, backs up that supposition. As we are seeing through their life stories, many of the greatest Christians of the last century have been single.

Actual outright discrimination is less common than it once was, but does still occur. It's sad and unscriptural. More common is simply bias or pressure by those in a position of authority.

The first thing to do is to go directly to the highest authority figure in the organization that you have access to, someone who can clearly speak on policy matters. Just ask them what their policy is. Get it straight from the horse's mouth, so that there is no misunderstanding. It may just be rumors or distortion, and there's no need to get upset over nothing.

Ask for a biblical reason if they are clearly treating singles different than married people. Be polite and leaders will often work to correct mistakes, especially if it is because someone under them has been abusing power.

Simply consider going elsewhere if an organization is going to treat singles like older teenagers or 2nd class citizens. Life's too short to kick against the goad, when there are plenty of other churches and organizations which are eager for singles to dive in. God opens

Meddling (Theirs)

windows when he closes doors.

Sometimes God calls us to service which may take extensive education, relocation, or years of preparation. It is not out of line to ask about an organization's policies before spending several years preparing. It isn't a fun thing to get a degree in a specialized subject and then be told that we cannot serve in that capacity unless we are married. Ask first and see ahead of time if the organization is going to be a good fit.

In the end, we are the sole people who can live our lives. Marriage is between a man and a woman, and God. We have already discussed that marrying is fine and not marrying is fine. This is an area where no one should accept meddling pressure in one direction or the other. Do what you want and God wills.

Chapter 10: Meddling (Ours)

- ✟ The four of them were a tight-knit group of girl-friends, who did everything together. Then Julie started dating Robert, who was active in the church. None of the group really knew him, but snide remarks and insinuations became all Julie heard from her friends. Gradually she came to accept everything they said about him. Finally, after a wonderful month she suddenly dumped him, leaving Robert bewildered and hurt. He just didn't understand. What had he done wrong?
- ✟ Ruth had been out all night on a hot date. Naomi was waiting up. When Ruth came in, Naomi asked, "How did it go?" Then Ruth told her everything Boaz had done for her.

God recognizes that being an older single is a lot harder than being single when we are twenty. He loves us so much that he gave us an entire book to help us out. The book of Ruth is a great story for older singles, with lots to teach us.

One thing Ruth 3:16 makes clear is that everyone's friends and family want to be kept in the loop on the latest romance. Admit it. We all like to meddle with our friends' love lives. We love them and we want the best for them.

We've just seen, though, that meddling is sinful, and we all know how much it hurts when others do it to us. Where do we draw an appropriate line?

The closer and more intimate we are with one another, the closer this line can be drawn. In general, realize that what hurts us is likely to hurt other singles, and just keep our mouths shut. But what about when it is our closest friend?

It's a tough call. Meddling hurts. It can end friendships and relationships. On the other hand, playing some small roll in helping two friends come together can be one of the most loving things we can do for a friend.

The best answer is simply to respect their wishes. Do we know them close enough to know that they are looking for that someone else? Then pointing out that so and so seems interested in them isn't untoward. But if we know they aren't interested in a relationship, then we should respect their wishes and not pester them.

Likewise, if we have direct knowledge that someone has a serious issue, then the loving thing to do is to share that knowledge. But only if we know a person well. Only if we love them enough to risk our friendship with them. We need to give this kind of situation serious prayer and thought before speaking.

If we don't know a person well, but just resent their intrusion into our pre-existing friendship, then this puts us at serious danger of meddling. Yes, someone dating has less time to spend with us than they once did. Yes, they may withdraw from some activities we once shared. But this is (within reasonableness) normal. Accept it and be thankful that God is gracing our friend with a loving relationship.

When a couple gets together, they often keep it quiet for a brief period of time while they try to figure out where a relationship is going. But after that, if we truly are close friends and care for them, then like Naomi, let's expect to hear how it's going. Give them someone to rejoice with! Positive encouragement is always welcome.

Sometimes, friends just need to talk and unburden themselves. It is an honor that they trust us enough to share with us. Just listen, cry, or pray with them. And keep our mouths shut afterwards.

Chapter 11: Lust

In Christopher Stasheff's novel, *Her Majesty's Wizard*, the hero encounters a priest named Father Brunel who lusts for a local witch. Though he has never had sex with her – or any woman – Father Brunel excoriates himself as a horrible sinner since puberty. Thirteen times he has left his village church to go to her, always to repent and back out at the last minute, despite her temptations.

Even without the act of fornication, Father Brunel's entire life has been ruled by the guilt of his lust. He dubiously reasons by the traditional church definition of mortal sin: that fornication is a serious sin, that he has knowledge of its seriousness, and that he shows his will to do it by leaving the village to seek out the witch. His life is lived in complete bondage to a sin that he has never actually committed.

My friend Edward has cable TV, then he gets rid of it for a few months. Then he gets it again. Andy does the same with his home Internet connection. Another friend, Alice, avidly consumes romance novels, then throws each away in disgust at herself. Each of these friends of mine feels ruled by their "secret" and oh, so serious sin.

Most of us are as aware of our own sexuality and that of others as is Father Brunel. From puberty forward guys are immediately aware when any woman enters the room. In our thirties and forties we are perhaps just as aware but hide it better. Sometimes we feel like our bodies' sexual urges are not much lessened with age, but we've improved our coping skills and ability to deal with it appropriately.

Lust

Wikipedia defines lust as, "any intense desire or craving for self gratification"[9], and also notes that the Greek word which translates as lust, epithymia (επιθυμια), is also translated as "to covet". Dictionary.com adds that it is "uncontrolled or illicit sexual desire or appetite; lecherousness"[10].

Most of the passages in the New Testament which mention lust fall into one of two categories. The first is the lists of sins to be avoided, which list lust, sexual immorality, debauchery, shameful passion, evil desire, and the like along with greed, drunkenness, idolatry, and a host of other sins (Romans 1:26-32; 1st Corinthians 5:11-13; Colossians 3:5; Galatians 5:19-21; 2nd Timothy 3:2-5; 1st Peter 4:3-4; lust doesn't make the cut in 1st Corinthians 6:9 or Revelation 21:8, although physical sexual actions do). These tell us that lust is wrong, but don't delve into any detail on it.

A little bit of detail would be most helpful, too. Many of us are so aware of our bodies and our sexual feelings – and have heard so many sermons and lessons on lust – that we are just as quick to convict ourselves as was Father Brunel. We know we are sinners: frustrated, horny, deeply depraved, and ridden with guilt.

Surely Paul hit the nail on the head when he said we burn with sexual desire (1st Corinthians 7:9 NET). But his answer to the problem was for us to marry, the very thing you and I have despaired of doing. No help there!

So we go through life feeling incredibly guilty. Never victorious. Always losing out to Satan in this, every man's battle – and many a woman's, too. How perverted we are and how unworthy! So many of us are downtrodden with this guilt.

And, no mistake, many of us deserve these feelings. Our consciences, prompted by the Holy Spirit, do in fact convict us of sin appropriately.

---

9 Lust. (2008, January 12). In *Wikipedia, The Free Encyclopedia*. Retrieved 02:06, January 19, 2008, from http://en.wikipedia.org/w/index.php?title=Lust&oldid=183807473

10 lust. (n.d.). *Dictionary.com Unabridged (v 1.1)*. Retrieved January 18, 2008, from Dictionary.com website: http://dictionary.reference.com/browse/lust

Lust

Some of us do need to take cold showers and change our hearts and our thought habits. Some of us need to treat our sisters (or brothers) with much more respect in our hearts.

Many of us, though, perhaps don't deserve these feelings to the extent that we sometimes imagine. Let's go back to the Word and see what the passages that actually talk about lust have to say about it. Matthew 5:28 is one of the least popular verses in the entire Bible. The Old Testament condemns adultery and fornication, but here Jesus raises the bar in a huge way: *"You have heard that it was said, 'Do not commit adultery.' But I say to you that whoever looks at a woman to desire her has already committed adultery with her in his heart."* (Matthew 5:27-28 NET)

Both Exodus 20:14 and Deuteronomy 5:17 label adultery as a serious offense; it is punishable by death under Mosaic law (Leviticus 20:10). Jesus here says that if you look at a woman to desire to have sex with her, you have already committed a sin equal to adultery in its theological consequences. So one obvious thing about lust is that it is a "sin of the eye", or of sensory input. Another is that lust is directed towards another person.

In 1st Corinthians 6, Paul gives us more insight into lust:

> *"All things are lawful for me" – but not everything is beneficial. "All things are lawful for me" – but I will not be controlled by anything. "Food is for the stomach and the stomach is for food, but God will do away with both." The body is not for sexual immorality, but for the Lord, and the Lord for the body. Now God indeed raised the Lord and he will raise us by his power. Do you not know that your bodies are members of Christ? Should I take the members of Christ and make them members of a prostitute? Never! Or do you not know that anyone who is united with a prostitute is one body with her? For it is said, "The two will become one flesh." But the one united with the Lord is one spirit with him. Flee sexual immorality! "Every sin a person commits is outside of the body" – but the immoral person sins against his own body. Or do you not know that your body is the temple of the Holy Spirit who is in you, whom you*

> *have from God, and you are not your own? For you were bought at a price. Therefore glorify God with your body."* (1st Corinthians 6:12-20 NET)

Here we see that lust is a controlling sin of excess, and it is a sin against our own body[11]. Nevertheless, we again see that even though the sin is against ourselves, it is directed towards another person (in this case a prostitute). This fits well with the definition of "uncontrolled sexual desire" which we read at the start of this chapter. Lust is debauchery and excess or intemperate desire which rules over us. As a bonus, we also get some very valuable advice in this passage from Paul on the best way to avoid it: flee from it!

Paul also wrote about lust in 1st Thessalonians:

> *For this is God's will: that you become holy, that you keep away from sexual immorality, that each of you know how to possess his own body in holiness and honor, not in lustful passion like the Gentiles who do not know God. In this matter no one should violate the rights of his brother or take advantage of him, because the Lord is the avenger in all these cases, as we also told you earlier and warned you solemnly. For God did not call us to impurity but in holiness. Consequently the one who rejects this is not rejecting human authority but God, who gives his Holy Spirit to you.* (1st Thessalonians 4:3-8 NET)

Again in this passage we see that it is a sin of the body, but directed against another (in this case the brother through adultery). God wants us to control our own bodies and not commit adultery or fornication like the non-Christian. We also see that sexual immorality is a very serious sin. Rejecting this biblical teaching on it is rejecting God, not man.

The Old Testament is rife with examples of lust. One of the saddest is

---

11 What exactly a "sin against our own body" means - as opposed to presumably against someone else – is a theologically complex question. But one of the things is that the offended party is ourselves, as opposed to someone else. If I hit someone over the head, the sin is against them, not myself. They feel the pain. Many of us know all too well that the sin of sexual immorality is felt most keenly by ourselves. Others, such as children, pay the price as well, but first and foremost the worldly consequences come home most often to us as perpetrators.

that of King David, the man after God's own heart. His adulterous affair started with lust of the eyes:

> *One evening David got up from his bed and walked around on the roof of his palace. From the roof he saw a woman bathing. Now this woman was very attractive. So David sent someone to inquire about the woman. The messenger said, "Isn't this Bathsheba, the daughter of Eliam, the wife of Uriah the Hittite?"* (2nd Samuel 11:2-3 NET)

Now unexpectedly seeing someone naked isn't necessarily sinful. Even with careful control over our television and Internet habits, we may still occasionally be surprised by it. Putting ourselves in a position where we may see it, on the other hand, is playing with matches. Don't be surprised if we get burnt. Did it really surprise David that if he looked down into someone else's bathroom he might see a woman naked?

Nor is finding a woman attractive sinful. That's making a natural observation that is going to occur to anyone. But David's just thrown gasoline on the fire. Where he first falls into open lust is when he doesn't avert his eyes, but rather takes concrete action about it. David clearly dwells on what he has seen. He sends a messenger to find out who she is. This is open lust. The rest of the chapter descends into a sad tale of adultery and murder.

In summary, we learn from these passages that:

- Lust is a sin of the concrete. It is a sin "of the eye", of looking at and desiring another person sexually either in person or through pornography or erotica.
- Lust is a sin of excess, debauchery (excessive indulgence in sensual pleasures), and intemperance. It rules over the sinner.
- Lust goes hand in hand with actual action with another person. Time and again in the Old Testament it leads straight into adultery or fornication. It is the playing with matches that starts the raging inferno.

So let's be clear. If you are viewing pornography or are thinking about a brother or sister and wishing you could go to bed with them, you are committing the sin of lust. It is a serious sin, and you need to repent of it.

But if you are just intensely aware of the opposite sex, or have sexual feelings and urges, but you're not dwelling on them in a concrete way, then rest assured, you do not need to feel guilty. This is normal physical sexuality, not the sin of lust.

The writer of Hebrews says about Jesus,

> *Therefore he had to be made like his brothers and sisters in every respect, so that he could become a merciful and faithful high priest in things relating to God, to make atonement for the sins of the people. For since he himself suffered when he was tempted, he is able to help those who are tempted.* (Hebrews 2:17-18 NET)

and

> *For we do not have a high priest incapable of sympathizing with our weaknesses, but one who has been tempted in every way just as we are, yet without sin. Therefore let us confidently approach the throne of grace to receive mercy and find grace whenever we need help.* (Hebrews 4:15-16 NET)

"...in every respect..." "...in every way..." Consider what that means. Jesus was a horny fifteen year old boy! And a frustrated thirty year old virgin! He was just as aware of the opposite sex as we are. He had a sexual physical body just like we do. And yet through all of it, he did not sin.

This means two things. First, it implies that our bodies' feelings and urges are not – in and of themselves – sinful. So we do not need to feel guilty over them. Secondly, and far more importantly, it means that he knows what we are going through and can both help us when tempted and give us mercy and grace when we stumble.

After David's sin with Bathsheba, the next chapter (2nd Samuel 12) is the story of David's repentance and God's forgiveness. God doesn't take away all of the earthly consequences of the sin, but he gives David grace. David went on to write Psalm 51, one of the best Psalms for any of us to read when crying out to God in repentance, turning from our sinfulness.

Lust

Satan would like us to go to one of two extremes: either be enslaved to actual lust, or be burdened with a load of unwarranted guilt we can't (or won't) get rid of, just like Father Brunel. Frankly, Satan doesn't care which we fall into, because either will stifle our Christian walk. But to struggle in the trenches, having victory more often than not and accepting the grace of God when we fall and need it, that's what Satan wants us to avoid.

After Jesus raises the bar on lust, he continues his teaching with this advice:

> *If your right eye causes you to sin, tear it out and throw it away! It is better to lose one of your members than to have your whole body thrown into hell. If your right hand causes you to sin, cut it off and throw it away! It is better to lose one of your members than to have your whole body go into hell.* (Matthew 5:29-30)

Jesus is using hyperbole; he's not condoning self-mutilation. But he is saying that it may take some significant sacrifice to avoid lust.

Anyone who has ever dealt with a computer knows, "Garbage In, Garbage Out". Our brain is no different. We are all different and have different love languages and things that "do it" for us. Some of us are very visual and find pornography very enticing. Others get the same charge from erotic "literature" or "music". So there is no "one size fits all" guideline for how to reduce our sexual temptation. But clearly making some lifestyle changes can significantly lessen the temptation to lust.

The two biggest sources of garbage coming into our lives are television and the Internet. Television is "push" technology which barges into our living rooms with its ideas of sexuality. Much of it is pure garbage. Give it up. And especially give up cable.

Is that suggestion radical? Is it tearing off an appendage like Jesus suggested? It's both a time consumer/waster and a source of poison slipping into our eyes and ears. Most singles watch way too much. It is impossible to watch television today without absorbing sexual imagery.

Now media is not in and of itself sinful. But all too often it is. And you may find giving cable up less of a sacrifice than you imagine. There are several excellent DVD rent-by-mail companies which are priced less than cable television. They have every movie imaginable and new television shows, a season or so behind broadcast; a far better selection than cable. With most plans, you are limited as a practical matter to 3-5 DVDs per week and there are no commercials, which means you can watch a full hour show in forty-five minutes. Most importantly <u>you</u> decide what comes into your home.

The Internet is a "pull" technology where we have quite a bit more control over which sites we view. There is no simple solution like DVD rentals. Some find smut-stopping software useful; I am skeptical of it, both technologically and philosophically. Others with roommates put the computer in a common room where there is no privacy. Still others find that they must forgo home Internet access. Figure out what guards your eyes and do it!

Despite our best efforts, we may occasionally be confronted by sensual imagery when we do not expect it. The Superbowl may flash a woman's breast. Or a work associate may lean forward innocently, giving us a view that we find intoxicating. Our last defense is averting the eyes. This is a difficult skill to develop. It takes strong self control. It is easier if our hearts are in the right place and if we have controlled our eyes in other ways.

Giving up cable and broadcast TV wasn't a huge sacrifice for me, but after about three months it made a big difference in my thought life. Take responsibility for your own input-output. Make whatever changes you need to in order to guard against lust of the eye. Paul tells Timothy in 1st Timothy 5:1-2 to treat our younger men as brothers and women as sisters, with absolute purity. Enough said!

Chapter 12: Masturbation

To riff off of an old marine drill sergeant, "95% of the people reading this book masturbate. The other 5% are liars."

Nothing else inspires such a load of guilt and self-loathing within us. Nothing else shames us as much. Nothing else is as embarrassing and unmentionable. Nothing else is taught about less by our pastors.

Many people come at this topic with strong preconceptions. As with the rest of this book, our study of this topic is going to be firmly grounded in Scripture. Here is everything that the Bible has to say about masturbation:

> If you have just flipped to this chapter because you are looking for teaching on an embarrassing topic, that's fine! There's nothing wrong with that. However, please read the preceding chapter before diving into this one. You will need that foundation in order to understand this discussion.

Masturbation

(This page intentionally left blank.)

Masturbation

That's it! Nothing. Nada. Zilch. The Bible does not mention masturbation even once. But we're going to take some time to look at some passages which are sometimes mentioned in connection with the topic.

The most commonly mentioned, Genesis 38:6-10, is the story of Onan and has been used by some to condemn masturbation.

> *Judah acquired a wife for Er his firstborn; her name was Tamar. But Er, Judah's firstborn, was evil in the Lord's sight, so the Lord killed him. Then Judah said to Onan, "Have sexual relations with your brother's wife and fulfill the duty of a brother-in-law to her so that you may raise up a descendant for your brother." But Onan knew that the child would not be considered his. So whenever he had sexual relations with his brother's wife, he withdrew prematurely so as not to give his brother a descendant. What he did was evil in the Lord's sight, so the Lord killed him too.* (Genesis 38:6-10 NET)

Even the briefest reading of this passage quickly shows that it is clearly referring to coitus interruptus (withdrawing prior to ejaculation during actual intercourse), and doesn't even condemn that practice, but rather the repeated failure of Onan to do his familial duty. Regardless of a person's views on masturbation, using this passage to condemn it is misapplying the Word of God.

The Old Testament does not shy away from controversy or embarrassing topics. The Torah delves in detail into such topics as women's periods (Leviticus 15:19-24), and cleanliness when defecating (Deuteronomy 23:12-14). It talks about diseases of the genitals (Leviticus 15:1-15). There is an entire chapter devoted to zits, acne, and skin diseases (Leviticus 13).

There are two places where the Old Testament does talk about semen emissions in general. In Deuteronomy 23:10-11 it says, *"If there is someone among you who is impure because of some nocturnal emission, he must leave the camp; he may not reenter it immediately. When evening arrives he must wash himself with water and then at sunset he may reenter the camp."* (NET) The Net Bible translation note on this passage says, "The Hebrew term (qareh) merely means 'to happen' so the phrase here is euphemistic (a 'night happening') for some kind of bodily emission such as excrement or semen. Such otherwise normal physical functions rendered one ritually unclean whether accidental or not." The NIV, NASB, and NET all translate this as "nocturnal emission".

The other passage says, *"When a man has a seminal emission, he must bathe his whole body in water and be unclean until evening, and he must wash in water any clothing or leather that has semen on it, and it will be unclean until evening. When a man has sexual intercourse with a woman and there is a seminal emission, they must bathe in water and be unclean until evening."* (Leviticus 15:16-18 NET) Here the Hebrew says "a man when a lying of seed goes out of him", speaking more generally of any semen, regardless of the "how". The NIV translates it "emission of semen" while the NASB sticks with the NET "seminal emission".

In both of these cases, what Scripture says is semen is to be washed off and makes anyone or anything unclean until evening. It doesn't really address in any way at all how it got there or any actions. The theological concept of clean and unclean is too complex for a discussion here, but it is not equivalent to our concept of sin. For example, Leviticus 15:16-18 above has been generally understood by observant Jews to mean that any ejaculation – including normal sex between a husband and wife – renders both people ceremonially unclean[12]. Yet neither Christians nor Jews believe that sex between a husband and wife is sinful.

So, the Old Testament does not speak about masturbation at all. But a reasonable Old Testament extrapolation can perhaps be made from Leviticus 15. Right after the verses about semen emission is a section on menstruation. Immediately we see a clear difference between the concept of unclean and sinful. A woman's period – which surely is not sinful since it is biological and she has no control over it – renders her unclean. It is, perhaps, not stretching too far to draw an analogy

---

12 The primary reason for this was to absolutely break the link between sex and worship. Many of the Canaanite fertility cults' worship practices were centered around sex. God said any sex rendered a person unclean until evening. Jews were not allowed to enter the tabernacle when unclean. This prevented them from perverting their own worship of the LORD by mixing it with pagan rituals.

Masturbation

between masturbation and a woman's period in the sense that it is a natural life function that can be messy and somewhat embarrassing, and that should be private, but that isn't per-se sinful in the Old Testament.

Ladies, all of this has been talking about male actions and semen. Apart from a poetic passage in Song of Solomon which may or may not describe female masturbation, or an erotic dream, or actual sex, or some really esoteric allegory of God and the Church, depending upon how you want to interpret the poetry, the Old Testament says absolutely nothing relevant to you. So you could draw one of two conclusions: either God doesn't care anything about it one way or the other in the Old Testament, and so you can do what you like (but we haven't hit the New Testament yet, so this story isn't finished...), or you can generalize from the view for men, meager as it is.

But the Old Testament is primarily concerned with externalities. The New Testament is much more interested in internals. It, like the Old Testament, is completely silent about the act of masturbation. But as we saw in the last chapter, it has a great deal to say about lust and sexual immorality (as does the Old Testament, for that matter).

Some simply pronounce masturbation forbidden on the principle that it is a hint of sexual immorality (*"But among you there must not be even a hint of sexual immorality, or of any kind of impurity, or of greed, because these are improper for God's holy people."* Ephesians 5:3 in the New International Version). Even if masturbation without lust is possible, it is nevertheless cutting close to the wind and certainly has a "hint" of sexual immorality about it.

A problem with that application is that both the New American Standard Bible (*"But immorality or any impurity or greed must not even be named among you, as is proper among saints;"*) and the New English Translation (*"But among you there must not be either sexual immorality, impurity of any kind, or greed, as these are not fitting for the saints."*) are more literal than the New International Version, and neither of them has that same emphasis on "hint of sexual immorality"; nor does the Greek.

In short, the passage simply doesn't have that meaning; it says that sexual immorality and impurity are forbidden, completely consistent with all the other Scriptures that we have explored. That is a far cry from the broad brushed "hint" which could include nearly anything from dancing to television to low-cut dresses, or nearly anything else the speaker disagrees with in modern culture.

We've already seen that God calls a concrete desire for sex with another person (aside from a spouse) sinful lust. That desire is typically driven by sensory input (the sin of the eye). It is intemperate, ruling over the sinner.

Sounds a lot like what many of us think about when we masturbate... Indeed, if masturbation is accompanied by pornography then it is like throwing gasoline on an already roaring bonfire. The same is true if it is accompanied by fantasies about our friends or acquaintances; we should be treating them as sisters or brothers, not objects of desire!

Also, lust (especially accompanied by pornography) tends to be addictive. It can rule over our lives if we let it. As we read already, Paul says, *"'All things are lawful for me' – but not everything is beneficial. 'All things are lawful for me' – but I will not be controlled by anything."* (1st Corinthians 6:12 NET) Lust is an enemy of temperance.

If masturbation is not mixed with concrete sexual fantasies and is done in moderation, then it is not sinful. But we must not be controlled by it. Can that even be done? It certainly isn't easy.

This is an area of no clear boundaries. Many teachers avoid giving any advice at all. But we need guidance. We are confronted with this issue, daily. It is our body. We can not flee from it as Paul advised, so this is one battle that we must fight the hard way; we should not fight it blind. We are venturing into areas that are the "fearful" in "fearfully and wonderfully made" (Psalm 139:14). It is exceedingly easy to fall into lust while masturbating. Indeed, it is probably commonplace.

There are several things which we can do to help lessen this risk:

We must avoid pornography. And not just when masturbating, but at all times, so that it isn't even in our heads. Not only is it directly lustful, but it has a half-life in our minds like radioactive sludge. It will eventually fade, but until then it makes it much easier for lustful thoughts to pop into our heads.

Masturbation

We can refuse to allow masturbation to control us. Our bodies have hormones which grow most insistent on a more or less regular basis, but we do not have a physical need for constant masturbation. We may find it exceedingly difficult to banish our urges entirely, but we may certainly control them. Lust gains a much easier foothold when the masturbation is for our own pleasure rather than at hormonal urging.

We can focus on our own bodies rather than others'. Masturbation is pleasurable and brings a wave of feelings. Letting our minds concentrate on our own feelings helps us to avoid slipping into lust for other people.

Lastly – and probably most usefully – we can store up good thoughts in the storehouse of our mind:

> *Therefore, if you have been raised with Christ, keep seeking the things above, where Christ is, seated at the right hand of God. Keep thinking about things above, not things on the earth, for you have died and your life is hidden with Christ in God. When Christ (who is your life) appears, then you too will be revealed in glory with him.* (Colossians 3:1-4 NET)

Paul returns to this theme again and again when discussing sexual immorality. When we keep earnestly seeking God, it will be reflected in our thought life throughout the day. And it will make it easier to avoid falling into lust regardless of what we are doing.

This and the chapter on lust have been difficult and embarrassing to write. And perhaps embarrassing for you to read. These chapters will probably offend some people. That's ok; you do not have to agree with me. Don't trust me; trust the Bible. Read it and judge for yourself. This is an area with no easy answers, where devout people can honestly differ.

> *"Finally, brothers and sisters, whatever is true, whatever is worthy of respect, whatever is just, whatever is pure, whatever is lovely, whatever is commendable, if something is excellent or praiseworthy, think about these things."* (Philippians 4:8 NET)

Now let's put this behind us and move on to another embarrassing topic that some of us struggle with...

Masturbation

> ✔ There are few, if any, good resources on masturbation that range any deeper than a brief superficial "Don't do it.", so study the one source that won't fail: the Bible. Read it, pray, and judge for yourself.

Chapter 13: Homosexuality

One of the nastiest things about being a long-term single is the people who occasionally assume that it has something to do with homosexuality. We live in a wicked generation which cannot conceive of celibacy for reasons of holiness or of sacrificing the pleasures of the flesh for obedience to God.

But in fact, some of us do feel more desire towards people of the same sex than the ones our mothers keep pushing us towards. If this describes you and you have chosen to abstain and ignore the world for the sake of Christ, be blessed. Great are your rewards stored up in heaven. You are not alone.

Celibacy sucks. No news to you. Well, Jesus knows. He asks nothing of you that he did not go through. He was celibate for his entire time here. And celibacy sucks regardless of whether it is because you haven't met the right woman or because you have no interest in the right woman. We are all in this boat together.

You have ignored the lies of this present world because you know God's word:

> *Do you not know that the unrighteous will not inherit the kingdom of God? Do not be deceived! The sexually immoral, idolaters, adulterers, passive homosexual partners, practicing homosexuals, thieves, the greedy, drunkards, the verbally abusive, and swindlers will not inherit the kingdom of God. Some of you once lived this way. But you were washed, you were*

Homosexuality

> *sanctified, you were justified in the name of the Lord Jesus Christ and by the Spirit of our God.* (1st Corinthians 6:9-11 NET)

You do not need a sermon on the evils of homosexual behavior. Such sermons abound, usually preached by men who have been happily married for many years. Their children attest to their sexual satisfaction. Easy for them to preach on this topic; their needs are met. But you need to understand the translation of the passage above because it can give a new way of looking at your physical urges.

The two terms translated "passive homosexual partners" and "practicing homosexuals" clearly in the Greek refer to the submissive and dominant partners in a homosexual relationship. Both are definitely condemned. But they also both clearly refer to active actions, not feelings or urges.

Do not accept the lie of the world that because this is "just the way you are" that it is Ok. But do not accept the opposite lie that you must feel guilty or condemned at your physical desires. Recognize that these feelings may be considered temptations just like the physical urges of a heterosexual, but temptations are not – in and of themselves – sins. We have already seen this in the chapter on lust.

Instead, consider the alcoholic. Nobody suggests that he does not feel the urge to drink; in fact, modern medicine has shown that alcoholism is often largely genetic. An alcoholic really does desire drink in a way fundamentally different than most people. That does not give him an excuse to drink, but rather suggests that he abstain from alcohol entirely. Even though he is around people who may drink in moderation without sin, he must abstain. Regardless, it is not a sin for him to feel the urge to drink, but rather to drink.

It is not a sin to feel your body's urges, regardless of whether they are for someone of the same or opposite sex. It is a sin to act on them. Don't let anyone confuse you toward either extreme.

Some teach that you may "pray your way straight". They have been portrayed as being more full of hatred than love, but the media is not trustworthy on this topic. The Bible is silent about this. I have no experience to guide you and so will not offer any advice other than to

Homosexuality

suggest that we serve a great and awesome God, he loves you, and prayer never hurts.

✔ Exodus International, at www.exodus-international.org, provides information and referrals to counselors dealing with homosexuality.

Chapter 14: C. S. Lewis

"Pain is God's megaphone to the soul."

Clive Staples Lewis was born in Belfast, Ireland, on November 29, 1898. While he lived much of his life in England, he loved Ireland his entire life and considered it his true home. When Clive was four years old, his dog, Jacksie, was killed by a car. He told his family that his name was now "Jacksie" and for the rest of his life, Clive answered only to "Jack".

Jack's mother died of cancer when he was only nine. His father sent him and his older brother Warren off to a series of boarding schools. He hated the first school which he attended; it soon closed and the headmaster was committed to an insane asylum. The rest were not much better. The students were preoccupied with increasing social status to the preclusion of everything good. They were brutal, and hazing, bullying, and pederasty were rampant.

Early in life, Jack learned that the only person he could trust was his older brother, Warren. As boys, Warren and Jack both created imaginary worlds. Warren's was modeled after India, while Jack's ran to anthropomorphic animals. Both of them had problems relating to their eccentric father. Warren and Jack remained close their entire lives, living at The Kilns together in later years.

Jack read voraciously, with a particular partiality to fantasy and science fiction (although he was not strong in the sciences himself). When he was a teenager, he discovered and fell in love with Norse and then Celtic mythology. He was fascinated by magic. At the same time, he was beginning a gradual drift away from the established church. By the time that he was 15, Jack called himself an atheist.

At eighteen, Jack won a scholarship to Oxford, but the First World War intervened. He arrived in the front line trenches of the Somme on his nineteenth birthday as a subaltern (lieutenant) in the Somerset Light Infantry. During training, he formed a pact with his roommate and friend, Paddy Moore, that if one of them was killed, the other would care for his family.

A year earlier, the British had opened the Battle of the Somme by losing more men in the first day than were in the entire American Army at the time. Five months after Jack's arrival at the front, the British tried to break the German lines again.

Jack was wounded by an artillery shell and evacuated to a hospital in England. Not only was he seriously injured, but he also suffered from shell-shock and depression. It was made worse by his father's failure to visit because it would have required him to travel from Ireland to England. But by December, 1918, Jack was well enough to be discharged. Unfortunately, Paddy Moore had been killed months earlier.

Back at Oxford after the war, Jack failed Algebra but took first honors in Greek and Latin Literature, Philosophy, Ancient History, and English. He was clearly destined for a career in classical literature. He taught, first as a fellow of Magdalen College, Oxford, and then as the first Professor of Medieval and Renaissance Literature at the University of Cambridge.

He spoke all of the major European languages – most fluently – and could not only read and write but also think in Greek, Latin, and a number of historical European languages. He published many scholarly works on medieval literature.

Jack also remembered his promise to Paddy Moore and cared for his mother, Janie King Moore, whom he came to refer to as his own mother. Later in 1930, he, Janie, and his brother Warren would all pool their resources to purchase "The Kilns", a house in Oxford. Jack cared for Janie Moore for the remainder of her life, faithful through her

C. S. Lewis

Alzheimer's and dementia.

By the time Jack was thirty, he had discovered the fantasy novels of George MacDonald. They and the historical writings of G. K. Chesterton gradually convinced Jack that God probably existed. After further deep discussions with his close friends, the Roman Catholic J. R. R. Tolkien and protestant Hugo Dyson, Jack became a Christian a year later. Of his conversion, he wrote, "I know very well when, but hardly how, the final step was taken. I was driven to Whipsnade one sunny morning. When we set out I did not believe that Jesus Christ is the Son of God, and when we reached the zoo I did." (*Surprised By Joy*, p237)

Two years later, in 1933, Jack, Warren, Tolkien, and Dyson started a literary circle called the "Inklings". Virtually all who drifted in and out of it over the next sixteen years would become successful authors. They met in Jack's rooms on Thursday evenings and on Mondays and Fridays met for lunch in a back room of a local pub.

Jack gradually became known in different circles as a successful writer of three entirely different genres. First, he was a widely regarded critic and scholar of medieval literature. He was the most popular 20th century Christian writer for his apologetics and his very approachable theological works: *Mere Christianity, The Problem of Pain, The Screwtape Letters,* and *The Four Loves*, among others. But it was his "children's" literature which brought him the greatest common fame. He is best remembered for the *Chronicles of Narnia*.

Mere Christianity popularized the Trilemma (though Jack never called it that):

> I am trying here to prevent anyone saying the really foolish thing that people often say about Him: 'I'm ready to accept Jesus as a great moral teacher, but I don't accept His claim to be God.' That is the one thing we must not say. A man who was merely a man and said the sort of things Jesus said would not be a great moral teacher. He would either be a lunatic — on the level with the man who says he is a poached egg — or else he would be the Devil of Hell. You must make your choice. Either this man was, and is, the Son of God, or else a madman or something worse. You can shut Him up for a fool, you can spit at Him and kill Him

as a demon or you can fall at His feet and call him Lord and God. But let us not come up with any patronizing nonsense about His being a great human teacher. He has not left that open to us. He did not intend to. (*Mere Christianity*, p.52)

In 1952, when Jack was fifty-three years old, he met Joy Davidman Gresham. She was going through a messy divorce from an alcoholic adulterer who abused her and their two sons (although she actually divorced on the grounds of abandonment).

Joy Gresham was the least likely person for a well known Christian author and Oxford don to get involved with. In addition to her divorce, she was a New York Jew who had converted from radical communism and atheism to Christianity in the late 1940s. She had published a number of works of her own and was well regarded as a poet. And she was seventeen years younger than Jack. Naturally, they fell in love.

Actually, they stealth dated for several years, refusing to admit even to themselves that their interest was anything beyond friendship. But they became inseparable. When Britain threatened during McCarthyism to deport Joy back to America as an ex-communist, it was to Jack that she turned. He and Joy were married in a secret civil ceremony in 1956, which granted her British citizenship.

But they continued to pretend to separate lives, telling themselves it was a marriage of convenience. What immigration authorities could not do, illness could. Joy had been complaining of hip pains for some time. She was soon diagnosed with terminal bone cancer. Jack could maintain the pretense of "just friends" no longer, and pleaded with a friend, Reverend Peter Bide, to marry them despite her divorce. The Christian ceremony was performed at her hospital bed about eleven months after the first ceremony.

The cancer went into an unexpected remission and Joy recovered. For almost three years they lived as husband and wife. They honeymooned in Ireland, took a holiday in Greece, and were happy, but at last the cancer returned and claimed Joy.

Losing the second woman in his life to cancer was devastating. Years before, his book, *The Problem of Pain,* was his first successful work on

C. S. Lewis

Christian apologetics. Now he had to find out if he could live his stated beliefs.

About a year later, a book, *A Grief Observed*, was released by N. W. Clerk. It was a raw and personal look at the experience of bereavement by a Christian. So many of Jack's friends kept telling him that he needed to read it that he finally admitted that he had written it under a pseudonym.

Jack lived only three years after Joy died. His death from a heart attack on November 22, 1963 was overshadowed by the assassination the same day of John F. Kennedy.

✔ *Surprised by Joy* is the great autobiographical story of C.S. Lewis's move from skeptic to Christian. Most of the many books C.S. Lewis wrote are still in print, and they tend to be easily readable.

Shadowlands, the love story of Jack and Joy, has been made into two separate movies, both of which are superb. Bring a box of tissues.

Chapter 15: The 40 Year Old Virgin

✝ "I don't want to die a virgin..."

There is something about the unknown that makes it incredibly enticing. Not to have known the physical love of another man or woman seems to be to have missed out on a major part of life. And a virgin is perhaps not a real adult, stuck in perpetual adolescence.

Don't you believe it. This is a lie of Satan. It is an incredibly effective lie because it is wrapped around a kernel of truth. I wish to God I could say I didn't know what sex was like, but I am divorced. I've had to discuss this with several prospective spouses and I'm so sorry for the disappointment it caused them. But as for you who have kept yourself purer than I, let me reveal what Satan won't:

Sex with someone else is great, no mistake; that's the kernel of truth in the lie. But not mindbogglingly so compared to masturbation. And after the honeymoon lust wears off, married people have a lot less sex than might be imagined, especially after kids enter the mix. So it may be better than masturbation in quality, but it takes two people in the mood rather than one. In short, you may be "missing" a little, but not a lot. Not nearly as much as Satan would like you to think.

Spiritual aspects aside, sex does not change you at all, in the sense of making you wiser or more "adult". Indeed, it can be the most adolescent act imaginable. Anyone who respects a sexually "experienced" person more than a virgin is a fool, pure and simple, in both the theological and the practical senses of the word.

The 40 Year Old Virgin

Your virginity – or your chastity if you are keeping yourself pure after a sexual affair – is your crowning virtue. It is something that no one else can take away (for rape is nothing like sex between two people united in marriage); you choose to maintain it against the flow in today's society. God bless you.

Your sexual history is your own and nobody else's, at least up until the point where you are talking very seriously about marriage with someone. Your friends or those in the locker room have no need to know your past. The phrase, "None of your business." is never rude. True friends build up the positives in each other; they don't tear them down. If someone humiliates you about this, ditch them. You don't need friends like that. There are plenty of people who will respect you and be your friend just because of who you are, not in spite of it.

If you do ever get married, your spouse is going to be so grateful and pleased with your self-control and purity. It will be worth every sacrifice just to present yourself to them, white as snow.

Many of us are never getting married. That's Ok, we've got a marriage feast in heaven where your sacrifice will be even better. Your robe that day will be pure virginal whiter than white. You will have earned the blessing, "Well done, good and faithful servant."

✔ Check out Revelation 19:6-9 for a sneak peak at what Jesus has in store for you!

Chapter 16: Rich Mullins

"Be God's."

Every couple of centuries, a new song joins *Silent Night*, *Amazing Grace*, and the Church's other great "psalms, hymns, and spiritual songs" (Ephesians 5:19) which will be sung for the ages. There is no debate over the Twentieth Century's great spiritual song. People will be singing *Awesome God* hundreds of years from now.

Its author was a rock star who eschewed fame and money, a man of sin and grace who focused on the love of God. He spent his last years living simply in an American Indian hogan and ministering to the downtrodden.

Richard Wayne Mullins was born on October 21, 1955 into a poor farming family in Richmond, Indiana. His family always called him by his middle name. Rich's father wanted him to be an athlete, but by age four or five, Rich was playing overheard hymns on the piano without sheet music or errors. Rich's family were members of the Quaker and Christian Church denominations, and Rich worshiped with both growing up. He attended Cincinnati Bible College, but didn't graduate. Later in life he went back to school at Friends University and graduated with a degree in Music Education.

In Rich's late twenties, and early thirties, he had a ten year relationship and engagement with a woman, but eventually his fiancé broke it off. He never considered anyone else. Many years later, he said simply, "The only woman for me is now married to another." That was that, so he chose to remain single.

Rich made the conscious decision to remain single, but that didn't stop him from feeling alone, even in the midst of his musical success and fame. Nor did it stop him from needing to feel loved. He deeply struggled with these desires.

His father was also a source of angst for Rich. His dad did not convey his feelings openly, never told Rich, "I love you," and for a long time there was a wide rift between the two. This bothered Rich deeply throughout his life.

Many people know of Rich's recording career. He played hammer dulcimer, keyboards, and many other instruments. In addition to his own records, he wrote numerous songs that ended up on others' albums. A hallmark of Rich's songs are the rich metaphorical lyrics.

But off the stage, Rich lived a simple life. After viewing the movie, *Brother Sun, Sister Moon*, Rich came to admire Saint Francis of Assisi. He modeled his life after him, eschewing the wealth and lifestyle of most rock stars. The profits from his musical career went to his church, which paid him the average U.S. salary for each year and gave the rest away to charity. Rich was deeply involved in Compassion International. In the final years of life, he taught music to children on a Navajo Indian reservation.

Rich's focus during his last decade was on the love and grace of God, the *Ragamuffin Gospel* message of Brennan Manning. Brennan's teaching was instrumental in Rich reconciling with his father shortly before his father's death.

Rich was always keenly aware of his own sinfulness, and *The Ragamuffin Gospel* also helped Rich come to terms with his failures. He said:

> I've been in and out of all kinds of things – like self-deprecation, self-interest, ego trips, alcohol, and other addictions. I've failed many times to avoid those kinds of temptations. But that's not what the devil was really interested in. What he was trying to do is make me feel apart from God. (*Praise Him!: Christian Music Stars Share Their Favorite Verses from Scripture*, Les Sussman,

p157)

Rich's last work was a concept album based on the life of St. Francis. His interest in the saint attracted him to the rich heritage of Roman Catholicism in his final years. There was no daily Protestant service on the Navajo reservation, so Rich frequently attended daily Mass. He never converted, and there is dispute over his intentions. Six months before his death, Rich himself said:

> A lot of the stuff which I thought was so different between Protestants and Catholics [was] not, but at the end of going through an RCIA (Right of Christian Initiation for Adults) course, I also realized that there are some real and significant differences. I'm not sure which side of the issues I come down on. My openness to Catholicism was very scary to me because, when you grow up in a church where they don't even put up a cross, many things were foreign to me. I went to an older Protestant gentleman that I've respected for years and years, and I asked him, "When does faithfulness to Jesus call us to lay aside our biases and when does it call us to stand beside them?" His answer to me was that it is not about being Catholic or Protestant. It is about being faithful to Jesus. The issue is not about which church you go to, it is about following Jesus where He leads you. (Radio Interview with Artie Terry, "The Exchange," WETN, Wheaton, Ill., April 1997, quoted in *An Arrow Pointing to Heaven*, James Bryan Smith, p54)

On September 19, 1997, Rich and a friend were headed to a concert when their Jeep flipped over. Neither man was wearing a seat belt and both were thrown from the car. A truck swerving to avoid the wreckage hit Rich, killing him instantly. He was 41 years old.

When Rich first moved to the Navajo reservation, he and his friends drove a 20 foot truck. When his friends collected his possessions after his death, they occupied less than half of the same truck. Rich had given everything else away.

Whenever he was asked for an autograph, Rich always wrote, "Be God's!" It summarized his philosophy of wholeheartedly throwing himself into a total commitment to God at every moment. If he was observing the moon moving over Nebraska or the flight of a pheasant, he gave God total glory in the moment. If he was performing before thousands, he gave God his all in worship. As soon as he moved off-stage, one on one with a stage hand he would give him his full undivided attention. Rich threw himself into total commitment to God as few did in the 20th century.

Since his death, there has been an attempt to turn Rich Mullins into a saint. He does not need it. He was both sinner and saint, and nothing could be said or written that would make him more of either. There is no evidence that he ever took formal vows of poverty or chastity, beyond what every devout Christian single willingly surrenders to God.

✔ The only book so far about the life of Rich Mullins, *An Arrow Pointing to Heaven*, by James Bryan Smith, is a good devotional hagiography, but not so great as a biography.

The Ragamuffin Gospel, by Brennan Manning, is not directly about Rich Mullins, but was extremely influential in his life and is an excellent read for anyone wanting to understand Rich better.

A Very Rich Project is a great unpublished underground MP3 collection of Rich speaking on a wide variety of topics.

The enduring legacy that Rich Mullins left is his music. Listen, worship, and be blessed.

Chapter 17: No hope?

> ✝ Karen is a really nice woman and a good Christian. She's bright, has a master's degree and is working on her Ph.D. She is a hard worker. But her nose, her round chubby face, her dumpy body... There's nothing she can do about them; it's just the way she was born. To top it off, she has bad acne. Karen has never once been asked out. Ever.

We – all of us, long-term singles – choose not to be married. Over one third of all Americans are single. No matter what kind of physical or emotional problems we have, we could find someone desperate enough to marry us, if we were really willing to lower our standards far enough. We have chosen singleness over the hell of an unwise marriage.

Some of us are looking for perfection, and do need to lower our own standards a little because they are totally unrealistic; the apostle Paul would not meet them.

Many of us, though, know what we are looking for and have reasonable expectations. We have not found mates because of physical, mental, or social handicaps. Some of us function perfectly well as productive members of society and the Church, but have social issues related to interacting with the opposite sex that are so deep that they are a part of us. Some of us – I hate to say it, but I'm being honest – are simply ugly. (There's a good reason there isn't a picture of the author on the back of this book.)

No hope?

Some of the people reading this book may not be getting married any time soon, but maybe, just maybe, five or ten years down the line someone will come along. They've at least got a tiny chance. A C.S. Lewis chance of an unexpected marriage late in life. Some of us know in our hearts that we don't.

What about us?

In short, it sucks to be us. We can let it drive us nuts, or we can get on with life. I hate writing this. God knows I wish I had some magic words to take away the hurt. I don't. All I can do is turn back to God. Hear what he told Isaiah:

> *The eunuch should not say,*
>
> *'Look, I am like a dried-up tree.'"*
>
> *For this is what the Lord says:*
>
> *"For the eunuchs who observe my Sabbaths*
>
> *and choose what pleases me*
>
> *and are faithful to my covenant,*
>
> *I will set up within my temple and my walls a monument*
>
> *that will be better than sons and daughters.*
>
> *I will set up a permanent monument for them that will remain.*
> (Isaiah 56:3-5 NET)

Today is the due date of my best friend and his wife's first child. Over the last nine months I have prayed daily for them. Before that I prayed for their conception. During the last week as her time grew short I have prayed often throughout the day. I am so happy for them!

And yet this passage of Scripture is like ashes in my mouth. I simply cannot understand how any monument could be better than sons and daughters. The Scripture doesn't seem reasonable on its face.

God is sovereign. All we can do is trust that these words written so many years ago are trustworthy. That's the only choice that we have. Despair, or the hope of a lost cause. Though even my own heart tells me I am foolish, I choose hope. I choose what pleases God.

Chapter 18: Coveting, Envy, and Bitterness

When I first confessed to my accountability partner (who is married) that I was really struggling with coveting, I could see the confusion in his face. It wasn't something he was expecting from me. I have chosen a less financially rewarding missionary lifestyle and live frugally. Then I tried to clarify, "I mean my neighbor's wife". Well, that really confused things. Now he thought I was talking about lust, which I could have been, but wasn't. That led to a long discussion.

Exodus 20:17 says,

> *You shall not covet your neighbor's house. You shall not covet your neighbor's wife, nor his male servant, nor his female servant, nor his ox, nor his donkey, nor anything that belongs to your neighbor.* (NET)

It wasn't easy for me to admit to breaking the 10th commandment. It took a while for me to realize I was sinning. But I do struggle with it. I see my friends' wives and children and, oh, I ache so much for them. I desire them in a family sense, rather than sexually. If I let myself, I think, "Oh, he is so lucky... Man, what I wouldn't give to be him."

The Hebrew word used for "covet" in Deuteronomy 5:21, the other place that the Ten Commandments appear in Scripture, means desire in the sense of sexual lust. But the NET Bible translation notes explain that the word used in Exodus 20:17, "focuses not on an external act but on an internal mental activity behind the act, the motivation for it. The word can be used in a very good sense (Ps 19:10; 68:16), but it has a bad connotation in contexts where the object desired is off limits. This command is aimed at curtailing the greedy desire for something belonging to a neighbor, a desire that leads to the taking of it or the attempt to take it. It was used in the story of the Garden of Eden for the tree that was desired."

We've already discussed lust, and that is not what we're talking about here. This is a very different kind of coveting sin, of envy. We see our friends' families and we would give anything to have the same love and companionship and children.

It really isn't difficult to understand why God forbids this line of reasoning. It quickly leads straight to bitterness, anger toward God, depression, and despair. Let run to its full conclusion, it can lead to really foolish deeper sins.

Now the temptation to have these feelings is fairly natural and even indicates that our heads are screwed on straight. But when they pop into our heads, following them or dwelling on them becomes the sin of coveting. When these thoughts appear, it is time to change the channel. And refocusing our thoughts is sometimes all it takes to get our minds onto more positive tracks.

It's even worse when someone we know gets married and appears happy when we know they are not right with God. Joshua Harris points out that Psalm 73 has a lot to say about this situation:

> *As for me, my feet almost slipped; my feet almost slid out from under me. For I envied those who are proud, as I observed the prosperity of the wicked... Arrogance is their necklace, and violence their clothing. Their prosperity causes them to do wrong; their thoughts are sinful. They mock and say evil things; they proudly threaten violence. They speak as if they rule in heaven, and lay claim to the earth... They say, 'How does God known what we do? Is the sovereign one aware of what goes on?'* (Psalm 73:2-3, 6-9, 11 NET)

Don't we all know someone like this, who is living in direct opposition to God's will? And yet they have a spouse and children that we would give anything for. Perhaps even a spouse that we could have had if we were a little less devoted to God and a little more willing to compromise.

Can't we agree with the Psalmist, *"I concluded, 'Surely in vain I have kept my motives pure and maintained a pure lifestyle. I suffer all day long and am punished every morning.' If I had publicized these thoughts, I would have betrayed your loyal followers. When I tried to make sense of this, it was troubling to me."* (Psalm 73:13-16 NET)?

"God, I'm the godly one! They are flouting you, but they get the rewards of a family and I'm left in lonely misery every night! This is useless. All the sacrifice of a celibate life is worthless. I should just tell everyone that I quit and go enjoy the pleasures of the world."

> *Yes, my spirit was bitter, and my insides felt sharp pain. I was ignorant and lacked insight; I was as senseless as an animal before you.* (Psalm 73:21-22 NET)

Our hearts and minds scream out at God. He made us this way! If he never intended for us to feel this way, then he should do something about it. It is so easy to be angry with God. It actually feels good to be angry with Him.

> *But I am continually with you; you hold my right hand. You guide me by your wise advice, and then you will lead me to a position of honor. Whom do I have in heaven but you? I desire no one but you on earth.* (Psalm 73:23-25 NET)

In the end, whom have we in heaven but the Lord? It is brutally hard to pray these words when in truth He is not the only one we desire on earth. The seventeenth century mathematician and theologian, Blaise Pascal, who never married, formulated what is called "Pascal's Wager". It shows that it is wise to follow God because if He exists then the reward is astronomical, but if God doesn't exist then nothing is lost or gained because it doesn't matter what you believe. Paul recognized this as well,

> *For if the dead are not raised, then not even Christ has been raised. And if Christ has not been raised, your faith is useless; you are still in your sins. Furthermore, those who have fallen asleep in Christ have also perished. For if only in this life we have hope in Christ, we should be pitied more than anyone.* (1st

Coveting, Envy, and Bitterness

Corinthians 15:16-19 NET)

Pascal's Wager doesn't apply just to heaven. We are rewarded even here on earth for following God's advice in our lives. Yes, we may not be on the heights of the great marriage that we wish for, but neither are we in the depths of hell that most of us already in one way or another have experienced that a bad marriage can become. The worst case scenario is that we are literally a hell of a lot happier than many of our friends who suffer through dysfunctional marriages and desperately wish they could be single like us. We all know that the wicked are doomed to horrible marriages behind their public masks; most of us have suffered through those types of marriages either ourselves or through our parents. It is far better to wish to be married than to wish to be single.

What's more, most local church leadership today, while they may be a little clueless about our struggles and needs, nevertheless do in fact recognize our unique positive position within the body of Christ. They may often not be there quite yet in how they go about showing it, but do not allow Satan to mislead you. They at least honestly desire more Christian singles to serve actively in positions of leadership and honor within the Church. If we let God, he will lead us to a position of honor even here on earth.

> *My flesh and my heart may grow weak, but God always protects my heart and gives me stability. Yes, look! Those far from you die; you destroy everyone who is unfaithful to you. But as for me, God's presence is all I need. I have made the sovereign LORD my shelter, as I declare all the things you have done.* (Psalm 73:26-28 NET)

At the end of it all, we are committed. God has protected our hearts from the worst ravages of marriage. In real life, as in Hollywood, the wicked ultimately get theirs in the end (about the only thing Hollywood has ever been right about!) To rephrase Pascal's Wager into Paul's terms, "If God doesn't exist, then we are really screwed." So he might as well be our shelter. He's got to be. We have no realistic viable alternative.

Whom have we in heaven but you, Jesus?

Chapter 19: Amy Carmichael

"You can give without loving, but you cannot love without giving."

Amy Carmichael was born December 16, 1867, into a well-off family in County Down, Northern Ireland. With her father's death when she was eighteen, the family's fortunes declined and they moved to Dublin.

There Amy began Sunday morning classes for the "shawlies", factory girls who wore shawls because they were too poor to afford hats and coats, and who were ignored by the established church. By 1889, so many shawlies attended Amy's classes that they founded "Welcome Hall" as a place for the shawl women to meet in worship.

On January 13, 1892, Amy was 24 years old and in poor health when she received a call from God to "Go ye." She developed a burning desire to go to the lost. Amy had heard famous missionary Hudson Taylor speak, and she first applied to become a missionary with his China Inland Mission. CIM finally turned her down because of her health.

This didn't stop her. Within a year, Amy convinced the Keswick Evangelical Convention to send her to Japan as a missionary. In Japan, Amy quickly started winning converts at a rapid pace, but she also was dismayed at the other western missionaries. After barely a year, her health disintegrated with neuralgia, migraine headaches, culture shock, and depression. Amy returned home disheartened.

But she was soon back in action. India was suggested as someplace with a climate more likely to be agreeable to her fragile health. In 1895, she arrived in the British Raj, or Indian Empire. Amy was 27 years old and she would never leave, working over fifty-five years without a furlough.

She started ministering to the poor women cast out and ignored by others. Soon she had formed a 'Woman's Band' of Indian women whom nobody else wanted. In 1900 they moved to a southern village called Dohnavur and started what today is Dohnavur Fellowship.

A year later, in 1901, Amy's defining moment came. A Christian convert brought her a small girl named "Preena". Preena was seven years old and had escaped from a Hindu temple. Female children were not wanted by Indian families, and so Preena's family had donated her to the temple to become a "davadasis", or temple prostitute. Preena's hands were already horribly burned from her punishment the first time she escaped and ran back home, only to have her mother return her to the temple. Amy became Preena's new mother.

Thus Amy found her life's work. Until her death, orphan girls and girls who had been given to temple slavery were welcome in Dohnavur. It was not always easy for Amy. Sometimes she would dye her Irish skin brown with coffee and wear an Indian sari to slip into a temple and rescue a child prostitute. Early in life, Amy had prayed that God would change her brown eyes to blue, but now she thanked God for the earlier "unanswered" prayer because she could blend in much easier in a crowd. She was frequently accused of kidnapping children from the temples.

Other western missionaries were aghast at her practical activism. For the next decade she was a pariah among the western expatriate community, who felt that she focused too much on a social Gospel. Her defense was that, "One cannot save and then pitchfork souls into heaven. Souls are more or less securely fastened to bodies and as you cannot get the souls out and deal with them separately, you have to take them both together." In 1912 her status was redeemed when Queen Mary recognized her for her work with the temple children.

A few years later in 1916, Amy founded "Sisters of the Common Life", a protestant missionary order of single women. She required a long-term commitment to singleness from all of the women seeking to serve with her. It was both a practical and a spiritual commitment. She firmly believed Paul's teachings about ministry being more effective without a spouse or family.

Forty years later, Amy encouraged one young recruit by recounting her own story of confronting God over her singleness while she was in Japan:

> On this day many years ago I went away alone to a cave in the mountain called Arima. I had feelings of fear about the future. That was why I went there – to be alone with God. The devil kept on whispering, 'It's all right now, but what about afterwards? You are going to be very lonely.' And he painted pictures of loneliness – I can see them still. And I turned to my God in a kind of desperation and said, 'Lord, what can I do? How can I go on to the end?' And he said, 'None of them that trust in Me shall be desolate.' That word has been with me ever since. It has been fulfilled to me. It will be fulfilled to you. (*Amy Carmichael of Dohnavur*, Frank Houghton, p62)

Amy was not all meekness and holiness. She had a fiery personality and could be imperious. In 1925, she had serious disagreements with an English missionary family that was working with her, and she broke all ties to western missions societies. The Dohnavur Fellowship became the first indigenous Christian mission in India to cast off western church oversight and funding.

In 1931, when Amy was 63, she was inspecting a building which was to house some of her workers when she fell into a deep construction hole. She broke her leg severely, dislocated her ankle, and twisted her spine. She spent the rest of her life in bed. This did not slow her down, however. She merely switched her energies to writing full time, as well as continuing to manage Dohnavur Fellowship. Thirteen of her thirty-six books were completed in her final twenty years, along with hundreds of letters.

Amy Carmichael died in bed on January 18, 1951, after fifty-five years in India. She was eighty-three years old. Her favorite phrase was, "You can give without loving, but you cannot love without giving."

Amy Carmichael

> ✔ There are too many biographies of Amy Carmichael to list them all. A good one is *A Chance to Die: The Life and Legacy of Amy Carmichael,* by Elisabeth Elliot. *The Story of Amy Carmichael and the Dohnavur Fellowship* is an excellent movie about her service and Dohnavur today; it is 50 minutes long and quite suitable for small groups. Amy herself wrote many books, most of which are out of print.

Chapter 20: Failure

- "No," the scorn and roll of the eyes said it all. Not just "No", but "No, if you and I were the last people on earth, the human race would become extinct. And I can't believe you even asked me. I am so far above you that it's embarrassing to be seen with you."

- When they stopped talking, that's when she realized it was really over. No more fights, no more yelling. Just nothing at all. He had written the relationship off.

- His new Christian friends didn't know he drank. For nearly a year he'd held out and not had a drop. Then on New Year's Eve, the first party he went to was with his old friends. By the time he reached the party where all of his new friends were, he was drunk enough that he didn't even realize how smashed he was. Afterwards he was so embarrassed that he moved to another part of the country, just to avoid them.

I was the last person in the company to know what was going to happen that day. The CEO called me into his office. My boss, the vice-president, was there, along with the company lawyer. "Stephen, I'm afraid we're going to have to let you go." Ten minutes later, they had escorted me out of the building.

Towards the end of the Dot Com boom, I left IBM for a startup company. When the Dot Bomb hit, lots of my friends lost their jobs. But I knew I was safe because we had cash-flow and were basically breaking even. Just another year or so and we'd IPO and everyone

Failure

involved would be set for life. We had just that week finished a major upgrade that I had been instrumental in leading.

Everyone said it was because of the economy. But I knew they were cutting someone after the upgrade was done just to reduce expenses and start making a profit so they would look good for an IPO or buy out. My boss had made the choice of who to cut because he felt threatened by my competence.

I had lots of reasons. And lots of angst over the next year or so. It was so humiliating and financially devastating.

But it wasn't the worst time that I failed.

The biggest failure of my life occurred when my wife drove me out of the house for the final time. The writing had been on the wall for a month (well, actually for years, but really openly and blatantly for a month). I had done everything that I could. But it was at an end. Even in my codependent state, I could see that to stay any longer would be counterproductive and just add to the pain, hurt, and sin.

Mr. Perfect Christian was getting a divorce. That evening, I flushed my life down the toilet. But what usually disappears in a swirl of water isn't too appealing. It hurts to fail. But consider what happens when we don't flush. Things start to stink. Bad. Flushing and cleaning the toilet keeps our house from smelling. Failure may hurt, but it opens up tremendous opportunities for growth if we allow it.

The classic role model for failure is Abraham Lincoln, who failed at everything he tried in life, except for being President of the United States. But we have no need to look to a married person for examples. Plenty of singles have failed.

Amy Carmichael's story is the archetype of many single missionaries. She started a great work in Japan, was considered a success by her peers and organization, and then before her first term was up, she burned out and returned home broken in spirit and body. This story has been repeated too many times to count since Mark quit on Paul and Barnabas during their missions trip in Acts 13:13.

But Amy didn't stop at failure. She went through a downtime of licking her wounds, prayer, and recovering her strength both in body and spirit.

Failure

Then she jumped back into action, and this time she learned from her mistakes. With what she learned from her first experience, Amy was able to have fifty-five years of successful missionary service.

John Mark, too, learned from his failure. In Acts 15:39, he is again back in action with Barnabas. But Acts 15 highlights the all too frequent penalty for failure.

> *After some days Paul said to Barnabas, "Let's return and visit the brothers in every town where we proclaimed the word of the Lord to see how they are doing." Barnabas wanted to bring John called Mark along with them too, but Paul insisted that they should not take along this one who had left them in Pamphylia and had not accompanied them in the work. They had a sharp disagreement, so that they parted company. Barnabas took along Mark and sailed away to Cyprus, but Paul chose Silas and set out, commended to the grace of the Lord by the brothers and sisters.* (Acts 15:36-40 NET)

Paul was not willing to trust Mark again after his first failure. This led to such a disagreement that it scuttled Paul's partnership with Barnabas. Imagine what Mark felt like at breaking up two friends. How humiliated he must have been!

But the loss was Paul's. Mark went with those who were willing to give him a second chance, and had his own long faithful career of service.

Years later, Paul counts Mark a coworker in Philemon 24, and then at the end of Paul's life, when he is imprisoned in Rome and the end is in sight, he begs Timothy, *"Get Mark and bring him with you, because he is a great help to me in ministry."* (2 Timothy 4:11 NET) Wow, what a change from Acts 15!

We need to become accepting of failure in ourselves and in others. What I flushed down the toilet became the fertilizer that God used to grow my Christian maturity. It took that stark failure to cut through my pride and legalism. It took the pain that I went through to grow emotionally. It hurt so bad, and yet because of it I am so much a better, kinder, nicer, person, not to mention a plugged in and serving Christian.

C. S. Lewis says,

Failure

> And Nothing is very strong: strong enough to steal away a man's best years not in sweet sins but in a dreary flickering of the mind over it knows not what and knows not why, in the gratification of curiosities so feeble that the man is only half aware of them, in drumming of fingers and kicking of heels, in whistling tunes that he does not like, or in the long, dim labyrinth of reveries that have not even lust or ambition to give them a relish, but which, once chance association has started them, the creature is too weak and fuddled to shake off. C. S. Lewis, *The Screwtape Letters*

Failure is only failure if we do not learn from it. We must get up and try again, learning from the past. Otherwise, as singles it is all too easy to slip into C.S. Lewis's Nothing as we let the years slide by.

The good news is that it is rarely "too late". Many singles are "late bloomers". Consider Betsie and Corrie ten Boom. Betsie was 54 and Corrie was 48 before they actually did anything substantial with their lives. Before that, Betsie had done very little with her life and Corrie had done a little service, but nothing extraordinary.

Yet Betsie became a rock like Peter and the last six months of her life shine like a supernova, while Corrie had another forty-three years of service to God! No matter what the past holds, it's never too late to leave Nothing behind and discover the adventure God has in store for us.

Ultimately, though, heaven doesn't depend upon whether we're a success or a failure in this life. There is no success big enough to get us into heaven and no failure tragic enough to disqualify us. All it takes from us is faith in Christ, as the GPL, God's Public License, reveals, *"For by grace you are saved through faith, and this is not from yourselves, it is the gift of God; it is not from works, so that no one can boast."* Ephesians 2:8-9 NET

Chapter 21: Loneliness

- It had been a long but good trip. As Tom and his business associate, Fred, walk out of the terminal, they are greeted outside security by Fred's wife and three young children. Fred kisses his wife, hoists one child on his shoulder and takes another by the hand, and they head for baggage claim.

  Meanwhile, Tom picks up his bags, walks out to his car, and drives home to a cold dark house. And the tears. Nobody cares. Nobody loves him. If he dies tomorrow, no one is going to miss him. When will this end?

- Jodie is the life of the party, a real people person. She's always having people over for Bible studies or socials. But there is a darker side to Jodie's sanguiness. Jodie cannot handle being alone. All the time she must surround herself with people. She is pretty and has no trouble getting asked out, but she has dated a long string of losers because she can't say no and risk being alone on the weekend.

  Fortunately, Jodie is wise enough that none of these relationships lasts more than a few dates. But she is getting more and more desperate for someone to fill this void inside of her. She can get frantic when she is left alone for even one evening.

Now we get to the real heart of the matter. Everything else that we have talked about in one way or another is impacted by the real issue we all struggle with: loneliness. If we cannot figure

Loneliness

out a way to deal with this empty ache inside of ourselves, it will eat us alive. It causes or exacerbates all of our other struggles.

This isn't exactly depression, at least in the sense that we have already talked about. Rather it's the hole in the water formed by a perfect cannon-ball off of the high-dive. It longs to be filled. It aches to be made complete.

Singles are far from the only ones who struggle with loneliness; marriage may fill a hunk of the void, but even at its best it is only a partial solution. As singles, though, we are the ones who face it in the most "in your face, can't be ignored" way.

Some "wise" teachers claim that before someone becomes a Christian, they are lonely because they don't have God, but after a person is saved and gets the Holy Spirit, they shouldn't be lonely. Any loneliness is just an indication that a Christian is still worldly and not spiritual enough.

I do not have to tell you that this is the teaching of false prophets. You already know it in your soul if you look inward. It directly contradicts what God said, *"It is not good for the man to be alone."* (Genesis 2:18 NET) That's as explicit as God can make it. Even if you are as spiritual as David or Paul, or as wise as Solomon, you are still going to feel this empty ache in your heart.

David was the strong and mighty warrior and politician, the man after God's own heart. Yet he cries, *"Turn toward me and have mercy on me, for I am alone and oppressed!"* (Psalm 25:16 NET) and *"Look to the right and see! No one cares about me. I have nowhere to run"* (Psalm 142:4 NET).

David's son, Solomon, wrote,

> *So I again considered another futile thing on earth: A man who is all alone with no companion, he has no children nor siblings; yet there is no end to all his toil, and he is never satisfied with riches. He laments, 'For whom am I toiling and depriving myself of pleasure?' This also is futile and a burdensome task!* (Ecclesiastes 4:7-8 NET)

And the mighty super-Christian, Paul, felt keenly alone as he neared the end of his life. He wrote to his protege Timothy,

Loneliness

You know that everyone in the province of Asia deserted me, including Phygelus and Hermogenes... For Demas deserted me, since he loved the present age, and he went to Thessalonica. Crescens went to Galatia and Titus to Dalmatia. Only Luke is with me... At my first defense no one appeared in my support; instead they all deserted me – may they not be held accountable for it. But the Lord stood by me and strengthened me, so that through me the message would be fully proclaimed for all the Gentiles to hear. (2nd Timothy 1:15, 4:10-11, 4:16-17 NET)

Like so many other lies of Satan that we've already looked at, this false teaching does distort a kernel of truth. There are two types of loneliness. One really is our hearts yearning to be closer to God; this loneliness is sent to motivate us to get off our butts and walk closer to God. The other kind of loneliness is more likely when we are walking right with God; it is our hearts wanting that deeper ultimate intimacy that not even a spouse can truly provide, that longing for the fullness of fellowship with God that will be ours in heaven.

Loneliness is at the center of all of our other issues. Now it's time for me to get personal. I have ached with both kinds of loneliness at different times in my walk with God.

During most of the Dot Com boom, I was a geek working for IBM. For three years I was technomadic. I had no house or apartment. I lived in 4 or 5 star hotels 100% of the time, traveling all over the U.S. and Europe getting large companies on the Net. It was a wild and gilded age, and the high point of my professional career. Everything was going right.

But every night I came "home" to a cold dark hotel room and was so miserable and lonely. I was a Christian, but I was wandering alone in the wilderness, so far from where God wanted me to be. (Ok, I wasn't alone at all; God was carrying me every step of the way, but that's a different sermon illustration for another time...) I was feeling this loneliness for a good reason. It was pushing me to get off my rear and do something.

One Sunday morning I got up early and went to church. The welcome center directed me to a room full of other Christian singles who simply wanted to be my friend. I had never felt so much love from God! I never looked back. This is the loneliness that God uses to draw us closer to him.

On the other hand, a few years later I hosted a large and successful Christmas party. I was a leader in a Christian singles program at a megachurch. For the first time in my life, I was part of the "in" crowd and plenty of people wanted to be my friend. I had dozens of casual acquaintances at my party, as well as a half dozen deep close friends. These were people with whom I had laughed and cried, vacationed, served, prayed, and worshiped. My house was full of people who genuinely cared about me.

I had a wonderful time. But after the party was over, and the last friend had left, I felt so lonely. I closed the door and the house was so quiet. The Christmas lights were still twinkling on the tree. I was on course in my Christian walk. And I was alone. I leaned on the closed door and prayed, "God, why? My days are vanishing year after year and I am no closer to a family. I am happy and surrounded by friends and walking closer to you than I have ever walked before, but I am so lonely!" There was nothing I needed to "do" spiritually, but I still felt this loneliness.

I felt like the Psalmist who poured out his lament,

> *O Lord, hear my prayer! Pay attention to my cry for help! Do not ignore me in my time of trouble! Listen to me! When I call out to you, quickly answer me! For my days go up in smoke, and my bones are charred like a fireplace. My heart is parched and withered like grass, for I am unable to eat food. Because of the anxiety that makes me groan, my bones protrude from my skin. I am like an owl in the wilderness; I am like a screech owl among the ruins. I stay awake; I am like a solitary bird on a roof.* (Psalm 102:1-7 NET)

Jesus has a reputation of being a people person; he was surrounded not only by the twelve disciples, but by throngs of thousands. Yet Jesus often spent time alone. Five times the Gospels record that Jesus withdrew to a lonely place to pray, in addition to his withdrawal to grieve when his cousin John was murdered. He was filled with the Spirit and yet he knew that he needed alone time to spend communing with the Father.

Loneliness

But more to the point, Jesus knew what it was like to be lonely when he didn't want to be alone. On the night that he was betrayed, he told his closest disciples, *"Look, a time is coming – and has come – when you will be scattered, each one to his own home, and I will be left alone. Yet I am not alone, because my Father is with me."* (John 16:32 NET) Even his best friend, Peter, left him that night.

At least he still had his Father. But Jesus has gone farther. He had drained the cup of loneliness to its last bitter dregs. On the cross he took our sin upon himself, and God can not look upon sin. As he lay dying, Jesus cried out, *"'Eloi, Eloi, lema sabachthani?' which means, 'My God, my God, why have you forsaken me?'"* (Mark 15:34 NET) In the end, Jesus died alone, totally cut off from his friends and his God. He knows exactly what we feel.

Yet God has promised not to desert us as He did Jesus at the cross. Even when everyone else has gone and we are all alone, God promises, *"I will never leave you and I will never abandon you."* (Hebrews 13:5 NET; cf Deuteronomy 31:6 & 8)

Everyone struggles with loneliness. A spouse or children may help with this feeling. But a spouse will only go so far towards filling this hole in our hearts. It is a god-sized hole and it takes a God-sized person to fill it.

Take heart, though! God planned us and desires fellowship with us. David gives us the solution of how to deal with this loneliness, *"For God alone I patiently wait; he is the one who delivers me."* (Psalm 62:1 NET) He knew that, *"The Lord is near the brokenhearted; he delivers those who are discouraged."* (Psalm 34:18 NET)

So use some discernment. If that ache in your heart is telling you to do something, visit a local church, talk to a pastor, and get off your back side and take some action! A month from now, you'll kick yourself that you didn't do so sooner! God so wants fellowship with you and between you and other Christians.

On the other hand, realize that nothing is going to fill this void completely this side of heaven. But don't despair, we are destined for better things. This emptiness inside will be filled at the marriage feast of the Lamb, when we see our God face to face and fall on our knees to worship Him.

Chapter 22: Ellie Grant Devore

Eloise Grant was born in 1924 in Cleveland, Ohio. She was active in the Highlands Christian Church youth program and was a devout Christian from a very young age. When Ellie was barely twenty she married a man who claimed to be a Christian. She should have known better by his actions. The marriage only lasted a short time before he ran off.

He had taken everything from her: her virginity, her self-respect, the respect of the community. She had always been the little prim and proper Christian and now she was stained for life by divorce. Good girls in the forties in Cleveland didn't have these kinds of problems.

It was a dark time in Ellie's life, but she gradually pulled through. Hannah, the young wife of the Highlands Christian Church preacher, Harold Blackburn, became her best friend and confidant. The Blackburns were the only ones that she felt comfortable being around.

In the 1950s & 1960s the Churches of Christ and Christian Churches were facing schism over the issue of congregational autonomy versus denominational structure. Highlands Christian Church voted to join the new Disciples of Christ. Harold and Hannah told Ellie privately that they were leaving Highlands.

To avoid splitting the church, they were going to start a new congregation on the far west side of Cleveland. It was miles from downtown, but the electric trains ran out to the western suburbs and there was talk of a new interstate highway system which would make commuting easy. The suburbs of Westlake and Bay Village were set for explosive growth and they would need good churches.

The Blackburns wanted Ellie to come with them to play the piano at the new Westlake Church of Christ. Since she knew that they weren't thrilled with the idea of even having a piano in the church building, she realized that they were offering her a place where no one would know of her past. She was very grateful. It was the start of the rest of her life.

On Sundays, the Blackburns would pick her up in their new car (put together in Detroit from parts made right in Cleveland) and they would spend the day at church and visiting people. After the evening service they would all go out to the local ice cream parlor.

Ellie gradually started taking a renewed interest in other things as well. She enrolled in Fin College. She could only afford a single course a semester, so it took her a long time to graduate. The only degree that they would offer someone with "her background", as the admissions lady delicately put it, was in Library Science. But Ellie had always loved to read, so that suited her just fine.

And she got a job working as a librarian at a large corporation. In the fifties and sixties, major companies had entire rooms full of trained accountants called 'computers' who spent their days doing bookkeeping. Some businesses had electrically driven mechanical calculators that helped, but it was still a labor-intensive job. They generated copious amounts of paper that had to be carefully filed for future reference in the company library. It wasn't terribly interesting work, but it was steady, fit well with her course of studies, and paid the bills. She still lived with her parents, so her expenses were modest.

As the wounds of Ellie's divorce receded into her memory and the scars faded, she began to take a serious interest in helping others. She started working with the girls at Christian summer camps. She could see so much of herself, just a few years earlier, in each of them.

It was at one of these Christian camps that she met and became friends with the Hostetters. They were raising money to start a new mission in Ghana, Africa. It was hard to raise the kind of long-term financial and prayer support that was needed. One evening as they were drinking coffee in the dining hall after the kids were put in bed, the Hostetters asked Ellie to be their forwarding agent.

Getting to and from the Ghana bush took weeks and was very expensive. The Hostetters could only afford to come back to the United States on rare occasions. They needed someone in the States to forward their mail, handle donations and paperwork, and visit churches and conventions to raise support.

After praying about it, Ellie agreed to take on the commitment of being the Hostetters' forwarding agent. Much to her surprise, she found that she enjoyed it and she was good at it. She really liked traveling to churches on the weekends and addressing ladies' groups about the Hostetters' mission.

Pretty soon, Ellie was carrying on a lively correspondence with missionary wives from all over the world. The letters took weeks to go and come, but she got comfort from the fact that she was these ladies' link with another female of their own culture.

By the late sixties, the northern Ohio Churches of Christ and Christian Churches were trying to reach out to the blacks of the slums of Cleveland. It was a very controversial action within many of the traditional white congregations, and Ellie found herself at the forefront of the effort. She stepped up to play the piano at the new predominantly African-American Southeast Church of Christ.

Ellie also hit her mid-forties in the 1960s and realized that she would never be a mother, nor likely ever remarry. It must have been a very tough time for her. She was very active in both the northern Ohio churches and in the broader missions movement. Ellie carried on a wide-ranging correspondence with dozens of missionary wives and had a ministry starting mission school libraries all over the world. Also active in in the civil rights movement, she had no trouble staying busy.

And yet she was so lonely. Nobody knew her past. Everyone just thought of her as the librarian who had never married. She had so much freedom to come and go that she would not have had if she had been tied to a husband and children. But she missed out on so much. At the monthly ladies' ministry meetings, everyone would pass a candle around the room and someone would blow it out and announce a pregnancy or a child's high-school graduation. But never her.

Well, menopause certainly provided clarity for her. She threw herself into service with renewed vigor. She bought Westlake Church of Christ its first organ, a move which nearly split the church between those from an acapella background and those from a musical worship background. They finally reached a compromise which pleased no one where it was played on Sunday mornings but not evenings. She also retired after twenty years and started a second career at the Cleveland Public Library. It was a low stress job she really enjoyed, and gave her the time for her ever-increasing missions activities.

At the height of the Cold War the Iron Curtain kept not only people in, but also Christian literature out. The move from providing books for mission schools to providing Bibles for persecuted Christians seemed a natural one. By the early eighties, Ellie was actively involved in smuggling Bibles into the Volga River Valley region of the Soviet Union.

In 1985, Ellie attended the Lake James Missions Conference, as she often did. There she met Dutch Devore. She already knew his daughter, Pat, a missionary with Casa de Ninos, a Mexican orphanage. Dutch's wife had passed away several years earlier.

The first time that Ellie stopped to get gasoline on the trip back from the conference, she discovered Dutch pumping gas at the same station. It surprised and embarrassed both of them when they ran into each other at the next fuel stop, several hours down the road. Dutch was headed to Pittsburgh and was planning on spending the night with Harold Blackburn in Cleveland. Ellie's oldest friends knew Dutch well.

At a ladies' meeting in the spring of 1986, Eloise Grant surprised everyone by blowing out the candle and announcing her engagement to Dutch Devore. The wedding of Dutch (age 65) and Ellie (age 62) was the social event of the century for all of the Cleveland area churches that Ellie had touched over the years. Ellie instantly became a member of the Devore family, with step-children and grandchildren. Dutch and Ellie enjoyed another decade of gallivanting around the world, visiting family and missionary friends before God called them home.

Ellie Grant Devore

> ✔ The other Christians whose lives we have examined wrote books or songs, have movies about them, or lived in "exciting times". Ellie is forgotten. But look how much she accomplished! It doesn't take a hero to do great things for God; it just takes someone willing to roll up their sleeves and allow God to use them.

Chapter 23: Stop waiting and live life!

The missions organization of which I am a part has a summer program for prospective missionaries. It's an intense week-long session on "Ok, if I become a missionary, this is what it's going to look like in real life to learn a foreign language, get used to another culture, or raise the necessary financial support." It is a wonderful time of praise and worship, classroom studies, and fellowship with missionaries from the field.

There are couples there every year that are both of one mind and heart and are ready to go, but inevitably there are also a few couples where it is pretty clear that one of them is gung-ho and on fire, but the other is really unsure about things. Or maybe they aren't even attending with their spouse at all. It is so sad to watch this play out. We may feel called to a specific ministry by God, but the sacrament of marriage takes precedence. It really is a joining of both sides in a union and partnership. This can scuttle ministry altogether.

And not just "go-to-Africa" missions. Any ministry with significant effort or commitment requires buy-in from both spouses in a marriage. When you add children into the mix, it gets even more complex.

Paul calls us out,

> I want you to be free from concern. An unmarried man is concerned about the things of the Lord, how to please the Lord. But a married man is concerned about the things of the world, how to please his wife, and he is divided. An unmarried woman

> *or a virgin is concerned about the things of the Lord, to be holy both in body and spirit. But a married woman is concerned about the things of the world, how to please her husband.* (1st Corinthians 7:32-34 NET)

God knew how much I would hate this passage, so Paul explains,

> *I am saying this for your benefit, not to place a limitation on you, but so that without distraction you may give notable and constant service to the Lord.* (1st Corinthians 7:35 NET)

I may not like to read it, but Paul knew what he was talking about first-hand. It was undoubtedly much easier for me to make the decision to become a missionary because I was single. I didn't have to convince a spouse that I had this calling from God. I didn't have to worry about pulling kids out of school. I just made the decision, sold my house, and moved half-way across the country. It may have taken a lot of prayer and work on my part, but there was no conflict or angst.

And I can give the ministry my wholehearted, undivided attention. While I do not normally work weekends, last Thursday I could decide on the spur of the moment to work next Saturday to revamp the office network because it had reached crisis point and needed to be taken totally off-line while I did the work. There were no worries about kids' soccer games or checking with the "better half" to see what she had planned.

A single missionary can often be two to three times more efficient than a married missionary. Not only is our schedule more flexible, but we need less support – a lot less than two people with children. Often a wife will want to help her husband in translation or ministry; she's been through a lot of training to get overseas and it's natural that she will want to make use of it. But that means getting someone to teach the children[13], so missions agencies need to continually be looking for a constant stream of short term assistants to come teach missionary kids for a year or two. Those people, of course, also need to raise their own support.

Do not misunderstand; I am not condemning marriage for missionaries

---

13 In many societies it would not be practical or prudent to leave the children with a national in this context.

Stop waiting and live life!

or anyone else. Paul makes it clear that they have the right to bring a spouse with them (1st Cor. 9:5). But Paul was stating a simple fact. We can often be more efficient in our ministries as singles. This is why Amy Carmichael required her missionary recruits to commit to singleness.

You too know of what Paul speaks. We are single. We don't make plans far in advance because we like to keep our options open. There's a lot of truth in the stereotype of us being commitment-adverse. Yes, in some ways that's poor life management. But it gives us a lot of power to do "crazy" stuff for God that married people couldn't possibly do without consensus-building, time, and perhaps argument.

It gives us the type of power it took Paul to do a total change of life and go from persecuting the Church to building it up. Can you imagine if Paul had been married?

> Honey, I know I've just come home from this business trip to Damascus... No, I didn't throw any more Christians in jail. I had this amazing vision. God spoke to me and now I want to sell everything and start doing missions trips!
>
> How long? Just a year or two in every city, maybe for the next thirty years or so. We'll get back to Jerusalem every once in a while. Usually just in time to get thrown in jail or start a riot.
>
> Oh, and by the way, if the Sanhedrin stops by, it'd probably be a good idea if you haven't seen me.
>
> I know you're skeptical about this, Honey, but let's pray about it...

Somehow, that strikes me as a tough conversation.

We don't have to worry about all of that. We decide to do something, and we do it. This is one of our strengths. Sure, there are disadvantages to singleness. But this is our advantage. Paul recognizes it and calls us to make use of it.

A powerful cure for the loneliness and depression of singleness is to do something intentional with your life. If you haven't discovered some great calling yet, pray to God. Ask Him to use you, and then get ready for a grand adventure. It may be at the ends of the earth, or it may be working with the poor or lost in your back yard. But God will use you for great things!

I don't know many Christian singles in their forties or fifties, but it has been my privilege to know several hundred singles living celibate godly lives in their twenties and thirties; a few dozen of them I have known quite well, living life together in missions or church single ministries. Most are now married.

The ones that aren't inevitably fall into one of only two groups: They are either maladjusted and needy, not really doing anything except existing; or they are busy doing incredibly wild things in service to God. The latter still feel lonely. Most of them still want to get married. But they are happy using their freedom rather than wallowing in it.

Ultimately, we may feel alone, but we are never truly alone. The last thing Jesus said in the Gospel of Matthew (Matthew 28:20 NET) was,

"And remember, I am with you always, to the end of the age."

Appendix A: For Pastors...

This appendix is focused on singles 25-40 without children because this is a large group that tends to be under-recognized. They often have little pastoral care and not much church teaching is accurately devoted to issues with which they struggle. Not everything described below is true of un-churched singles in general.

Chapter 24: Just how many singles are there?

A lot! 43% of all American adults are single and 31% of all households consist of nonfamily households, defined as either a person living alone or a householder who shares the housing unit with nonrelatives only – for example, boarders or roommates. This percentage is exploding, having nearly doubled between 1970 and 2000, predominantly due to more people living alone: the vast majority of these nonfamily households are men or women living alone. 47% of all nonfamily households are women living alone, while 34% are men living alone.

What about "alternative" lifestyles? Only about 18% of nonfamily households and a paltery 5.7% of all households in general. To top it off, that statistic includes any single men or women living with roommates, which means it includes many godly Christian singles.

By age 35, 26% of all men and women have still never married. Many more have become "single again". By age 65, only 5% of people have never married, but many more are living alone due to divorce or death of a spouse. *These statistics are from the U.S. Census Bureau's reports, "Facts for Features: Unmarried and Single Americans Week (2004)", "America's Families and Living Arrangements, 2000" and "Living Together, Living Alone: Families and Living Arrangements, 2000".*

So how many singles are there? Over a third of the population. Don't see that many in your church on Sunday morning? Maybe that should

Just how many singles are there?

be telling you something...

The Male/Female Disparity

When you think about the singles you do know in your local congregation, something else probably becomes very quickly evident: there are a lot more females than males. This is only somewhat true in their twenties, but by the late thirties and beyond the trend is massive and just snowballs over the years. There are at least three separate things that lead to a demographic tidal wave of ladies outnumbering single male Christians.

First, to begin with, there are simply more women than men. Females live significantly longer than males (5.8 years longer!). More male than female babies are born (1.05 to 1), but the difference is too small to make up for the longer lifespan. The United States had 6.1 million more females than males in 2000. (*Residence Population Estimates of the United States by Sex, Race, and Hispanic Origin, U.S. Census Bureau*)

Second, the American prison system makes these statistics even more lopsided. More than 1 out every 100 people in the U.S. is sitting behind bars right now. And two more are out on probation or parole. (*Prison Statistics*, U.S. Department of Justice, 2007) Whether measured in raw numbers or as a percentage of population, the United States has vastly more people in prison than any other country on earth. Indeed, the only nations in history that have ever exceeded the current U.S. prison population are Nazi Germany and Stalinist Russia.

Male prisoners outnumber females by over 10:1, meaning nearly 2 out of every 100 men are behind bars. A falling tide lowers all boats just as a rising tide raises them: this exacerbates the female/male ratio of single people who could be in your pews. Because African Americans are six times more likely to receive prison sentences than whites for the same offense, for blacks this distortion is much worse.

Lastly, Christianity has always appealed disproportionately to females more than males, primarily because – modern preconceptions aside – it has generally placed a high value on women. This has skewed its sex

Just how many singles are there?

ratio throughout its history[14] and is still true today. So more of those females than males will be showing up in your local church.

In summary, the pie of single ladies is larger than the pie of single men. The imprisonment of so many men cuts a hefty hunk out of what is already a smaller pie. And the respect that Christianity has for women means that a larger slice of their larger pie is going to end up on your plate.[15]

Why should you care?

God has given these people into your care. You're fooling yourself if you think they don't exist in your church. Though you're probably correct that they don't exist in the numbers or percentages that census figures would suggest. That's because they often aren't seeing much in the local church to attract them.

Singles are a great source of unreached people who need God and are ripe for evangelism. Unless you have a large congregation, it can be difficult getting to the first eighteen or so regulars in a new singles ministry. But once you do, something miraculous happens and it becomes an engine that starts running of itself!

Un-churched people start showing up left and right. They know they are broken. They have already been through the world's solution and found it empty. Now they are ready for God's answer.

Why do singles need their own ministry?

Why do teenagers need their own ministry? Or seniors? Or new parents? These are different seasons of life that have distinct pastoral needs and require some (not all!) teaching on special topics. It is surprising that this question even needs answered. Yet it all too frequently gets strong push-back when a singles ministry is proposed.

---

14 See *The Rise of Christianity* by Rodney Stark, for an exhaustive study of this topic.

15 For missionaries, the ratio is even more skewed towards females: There are about six single ladies on the mission field for every single male. And I still can't get a date...

Just how many singles are there?

Singles, too, have their own needs. For example, they need significantly more fellowship activities than most other people. They're going to get this need filled one way or another. It can be through the local church or the local bar; it's your choice which...

Some congregations maintain that they do not have a separate singles ministry because they integrate them into the life of the church. If this is how your church is organized, ask, "How's that working out for you?" A simple way to answer this is to see if your church's demographics reflect the census's demographics. If about a third of the people filling your pews are single, then you've done a good job. But often this is just an excuse to ignore your singles and do nothing to evangelize the un-churched in this demographic or to meet their pastoral needs.

Some singles will not want to be "singled" out in a singles program for various reasons. That's fine; nobody has to attend, any more than people with new babies have to be involved in the Children's Ministry or the elderly have to attend that Sunday school class that has been meeting in the back room for 30 years. They are all voluntary.

But your singles really do need care and feeding which they are unlikely to get in a general setting. They do not need yet another lesson on how to discipline their non-existent children; indeed, for some of them these lessons sear their hearts with unfulfilled longing. They do need to know how to appropriately express interest in someone of the opposite sex. Yes, that may seem an easy trivial skill for some people. But for many singles, it is an intensely embarrassing mystery that they have failed at time and time again. When was the last time you taught a lesson on masturbation? Or learning to trust again after divorce?

And there is something indescribable that occurs when someone has children. They change. It is a good and appropriate change. But a unique season of their life is over, and suddenly their social activities all seem to degenerate to talking about kids. This is a sure way to squelch your singles' interest in social activities. It is difficult to mix singles and young marrieds' fellowship activities successfully on a regular basis.

How can you meet these distinctive pastoral needs without a dedicated singles ministry? Just as importantly, how are you reaching out to the third of un-churched America which is single?

Chapter 25: The anatomy of your singles...

Divorce

The single largest common denominator among your singles is that nearly all of them are scarred in some way by divorce. Only about 25% have experienced it for themselves; most of the rest come from divorced families. Divorce is a ravenous beast that has gorged itself on American society. The singles in your church are the result.

Single people within the church are sometimes grouped by age into 25-39 and 40+. This is a pretty reasonable age break because a 40 year old and a 25 year old have little in common. Rightly or wrongly, these age breaks sometimes serve as code language for "never married or divorced with no kids" and "divorced with kids or single and really screwed up".

Loneliness

Christianity Today recently asked self-identified Christian singles, "What's your biggest singlehood struggle?"[16] The top answer was "Loneliness", with 34%, double the next two most common answers, "trying to trust God's will for my life" and "trying to be content in my current life stage".

Loneliness is the cross that all singles bear. It is the biggest problem for

---

16 Christianity Today, retrieved 5:01PM CST on April 3, 2009 from http://www.christianitytoday.com/singles/features/poll.html.

most singles. Some hide it more than others, and some deal with it better than others. But all singles really struggle with it. There are a variety of coping mechanisms, some more healthy than others. Many singles tend to move to one of two extremes, either filling every moment with social activities so that they are never alone, or withdrawing into a hard shell of aloneness. <u>Singles need significant teaching on loneliness.</u>

Depression and other mental issues

The second most common shared characteristic of singles in the Church is depression. About a quarter of singles are on medication or under a doctor or counselor's care[17]. Quite a few more would benefit from the same, based on fairly easy to see characteristics and behaviors.

Quite a few have various kinds of anxiety disorders, such as not being able to handle crowds or conversely not being able to be alone. Extreme personality types: choleric, sanguine, phlegmatic, or melancholy, also seem to be more common in singles than married people. Most of these Christians are no more messed up than their married counterparts, but many of them don't realize this and view it as a mark of shame.

Handicaps, excess weight, & ugliness

Some people are unlikely to get married because of physical or mental handicaps, excess weight, or ugliness. These people are not actually without hope entirely, but it certainly takes a special type of relationship in some cases. Despite what even the best people say, most people are driven at least significantly by appearance.

Those that can look past the ugly duckling may very well be blessed with a swan. It can be difficult to guess which of these romances will work out. God moves in mysterious ways. Thankfully, we are called to be witnesses, not judges or juries.

---

17 This number is a rough estimate based on experience; no definitive statistics are available from the Census Bureau or CDC, but several studies have found that - even when controlling for the factor that poor mental health may keep people from getting married - singles have poorer mental health on average than married people.

The anatomy of your singles...

Substance abuse and similar issues

Some people are single for a reason, and it is sometimes due to substance abuse or some other struggle like gambling, pornography, or Internet addiction. Don't make the mistake of assuming that all of your singles have issues like these, but a minority of singles struggle with these types of problems. Some of them can be assisted by involvement in a singles ministry, but many of them will not find a suitable place in such a ministry, needing instead more serious specialized help.

Despair

As years fade into decades, life can seem like a long drawn out race that will never end. As more and more of their friends get married (and have no doubt, within five years most of the singles that come through a singles ministry will be married – for better or worse), the remainder gradually come to realize that for them there may be no happily ever after. It is very easy to slip into despair when this finally hits home.

Giving & finances

Singles have a reputation in the church for not being givers. Singles fall into two categories financially. There are the perennial students who don't honestly have any significant money and there are the SINK professionals with a single income and no kids. These singles tend to live high on the hog; they own their own homes and have plenty of disposable income.

And yet these singles do not really deserve the reputation that they have. As a faith-based missionary, some of my largest supporters are singles. Partly this is because I have been active in a large singles ministry and know many. But I also know many young married couples. The married couples have kids and mortgages. They give, but only the single professionals have the high income and low expenses to give at a level equal to some older traditional givers.

And don't discount the students and working poor, either. I have been truly humbled by the size of the support I have received from some people that I know are not well off. The widow's mite could just as

The anatomy of your singles...

easily be the sixth-year grad student's. These supporters are wonderful and faithful!

Singles do tend to give a lot to separate causes apart from the local church. There are probably many reasons for this. One major one may be that they know they aren't expected to give as much in church. Another may be because they often would rather give straight to specific causes that they agree with than to a church's "general fund". If your church giving is lacking in either missions or benevolence, chances are that your singles are giving directly to causes which they believe in within those areas.

Commitment & free time

The stereotype about singles being commitment averse is largely correct, at least in general. And true at least as much about the ladies as about the guys. Singles, as a rule, hate to plan more than a few weeks in advance. Who knows what might come up? *(This is often a code phrase for "Who knows who might come up?")*

This is both a strength and a weakness. It can be frustrating when trying to plan. But it can give them wonderful flexibility to adapt to the needs of the moment. Got a last minute service project or a missions opportunity to go gallivanting halfway around the globe on a moment's notice? Call some of your singles!

Beware S.A.D.!

My Sunday School teacher is a young Missionary in Training named Bryan. He's intelligent, charming, and we are good friends. This Sunday morning he announced a class Valentine's Day dinner. Looking out and seeing me, Bryan wanted to be inclusive, "And it's not just for couples who are married or dating. It's also for those who... don't date. Er... You don't need a sweetheart to come..." Open mouth, insert foot. Everything he said just made it worse. Bryan is great and his heart was in the right place, but I still ended up feeling like a loser.

Many people know that those without families struggle more around the holidays. But you may not realize that **S**ingleness **A**wareness **D**ay,

The anatomy of your singles...

February 14, is the annual carpet bombing of most singles' self-esteem. The first half of February is devastating to singles. All of society screams the same message at them: "Failure! Loser! Reject!" Many are at their low for the year.

What can you do about it? Not much except prayer and giving us some extra grace: this is also a time of year when singles tend to make bad choices. Just enjoy this special holiday without rubbing it in our faces.

It can be a good opportunity for your singles to serve each other, though. If you've got some single men's groups and ladies' groups, consider encouraging the men to throw a fancy sit-down dinner for the ladies as a group to a group.

Other holidays that are particularly bad are Mother's Day and Father's Day. Singles are frequently embarrassed on these Sunday mornings by the handing out of flowers to mothers or fathers by those who assume that any adult is a parent. Many singles want children more than anything else except perhaps a spouse. To be handed a flower in these circumstances is like salt rubbed in a raw wound, especially for those in their late thirties and older.

Chapter 26: Teaching Singles

> *He told them many things in parables, saying: "Listen! A sower went out to sow. And as he sowed, some seeds fell along the path, and the birds came and devoured them. Other seeds fell on rocky ground where they did not have much soil. They sprang up quickly because the soil was not deep. But when the sun came up, they were scorched, and because they did not have sufficient root, they withered. Other seeds fell among the thorns, and they grew up and choked them. But other seeds fell on good soil and produced grain, some a hundred times as much, some sixty, and some thirty. The one who has ears had better listen!"* (Matthew 13:3-9 NET)

People generally react to Christian singles classes and groups in one of three ways: they visit once, leave, and never come back; they become a comet; or they dive in.

Those rocky ground visitors that never come back probably would not have fit in very well, anyways. The weedy ground comets are a tougher nut to crack. Most of them are struggling with some major character flaw. They will get their act together and be faithful for a month or two, then disappear for three or four months, only to reappear again suddenly. Sometimes some extra effort can help them stabilize their orbit; sometimes not. Ultimately, it is their choice.

The fertile soil seeds are wonderful to behold. They will energize your personal ministry and make up for all the rejection. They know they've found what they were (consciously or not) seeking, get involved, and never look back!

Most singles have been through some pretty heavy stuff before they show up at a Christian singles group. They may not be able to express it or realize it themselves, but they are open and ripe for major life change. Indeed, it is clear that God uses trauma to bring many people to a group where they can learn of His love for them.

When they show up they are hurting badly. They are the walking wounded of the spiritual warfare going on around us. Some of their wounds may be self-inflicted. And some have had unspeakable atrocities committed against them.

Many of these folks will eagerly dive in and get involved. Others will have to be gradually coaxed out of their shells; they know they've found a safe place to heal, but it will take some time. After a while of rapid growth and healing, most will gradually lead more and more. Their interpersonal skills will become better, and they will become more mature Christians by serving. Most of these people will get married within five years and become the "young marrieds" of the Church.

Some have been hurt so badly that they are not going to get married any time soon. This book is for them. Many of these are Extra Grace Required people, but some are jewels. And some of the EGRs will blossom into jewels with just a little time and love. Have patience with some and help others to grow in whatever special way God has intended for them. But don't let any of them waste themselves!

Find me a mate!

It can be tricky to find a balance in teaching singles. The 800 pound gorilla in the room is their singleness. Many of them think that you should be doing everything you can to get them a spouse. They're hurting and lonely, and they think that should be the focus of your teaching.

Indeed, it should be taught on more than it is. **You can not ignore their singleness and retain their respect.** But basic interpersonal skills like the Golden Rule are where most teaching for singles needs to focus. The Sermon on the Mount simply doesn't go out of style.

Teaching Singles

It's not all about sex.

Singles tune out any sermon on sex taught by a married pastor because you have no credibility to be preaching it; when they look at the pulpit, they see someone with a wife and children. Rightly or wrongly, they assume that means you have a healthy sex life and a loving, caring, family. Some singles don't have a realistic view of sex (or the lack thereof) after marriage.

They also perceive that you don't have a clue about their struggles. To judge from the little teaching done on Sundays about singles, most pastors think the main thing Christian singles struggle with is premarital sex. Nothing could be further from the truth! The same Christianity Today poll that shows that loneliness is overwhelmingly single Christians' largest struggle also reveals that "sexual temptation" comes in a paltry fifth place at 8%.

It is certainly true that a significant part of the human race – single and married – is promiscuous. The worldwide spread of HIV proves that, if nothing else. The phrase, "Everyone is doing it." may be trite, but it seems that to a great extent many people are in fact "doing it" outside of marriage[18]. It may be that many nominally "Christian" singles are also sexually active.

And yet the singles who are actually plugged into your church, most strikingly, are not. Let's repeat that explicitly because it runs counter to all perceived "wisdom": **The single adult Christians who are active in your church are rarely, if ever, having sex with anyone else.**

Do not misunderstand, lukewarm Christians or those who have just shown up in church may very well be living the lifestyle you stereotype. We are speaking here specifically of the singles who are involved and serving in your congregation.

Your singles are in an environment where legally they can have sex. Culturally they are actually thought of as weird or losers if they don't have sex. Society tells them it is normal. Their sexuality is questioned

---

18 This is somewhat misleading, in the sense that some people are quite active, while many others are sexually inactive. In other words, there is a large deviation from the mean in this area, even among non-Christians.

if they aren't married. Their own bodies urge them to have sex. And yet they have overcome the world!

The singles in your congregation have chosen a very tough course, for the sake of godliness. Stop treating them as if this were a major deal. They all know that premarital sex is wrong. They don't need yet another sermon to convince them of it. Instead treat your singles as the heroes they are in this area!

Is sex a temptation? Sure. Do some of your singles occasionally stumble? Yes. But no more so than married people. And far less than one might guess. Rarely do your single leaders stumble in this area. In honesty, they are defeating Satan far more often than most realize.

Sermon browbeating about premarital sex also isn't going to do much good with worldly singles, either. They may not know the Gospel, but they certainly know that "God hates sex." That's a message Hollywood has sold them and these sermons do nothing to change that perception.

Instead, how about a sermon on dealing with loneliness, or on living life instead of waiting on pause? Do you realize Jesus was a frustrated 30 year old virgin? Jesus's "creds" in this area are a lot stronger than anyone's who is wearing a wedding ring. Help them build a relationship with him and behavior change will follow.

Also, never assume that everyone has had sex. Or even that everyone has been kissed. Satan has made a mockery of the 40 year old virgin. But you have a few in your church. They are embarrassed by it and ashamed of what should be their crowning virtue. Praise them in general, but never put any of them in a situation where they will be singled out. A simple group icebreaker of "Describe your first kiss..." can be shattering to the person who has never been kissed.

You also have some singles who have in the past had dozens of sexual partners, abortions, STDs, and all the scars that come with them. You don't need to tell them how bad extramarital sex is, either. They already know it far better than you.

Raise their expectations.

Expect more from your singles in the way of serious service and you will get more. Teach on some of their topics. Mentor them and appoint some single deacons; singles have a serious need for single role models in the Church today. You will be surprised what they step up to. Don't let them be lazy in church because they are single and not "real" grown ups. This is a self-image with which they often struggle; work to disabuse them of the notion.

Everyone needs to feel loved.

One of our deepest inherent needs is to feel loved. It will drive us to do all kinds of crazy things (e.g., getting married!). Like many others, singles often buy into Satan's lie that God does not love them. Exercise great caution in how you teach on this.

For your singles this black lie is a thin veneer around a solid nugget of truth. Singles know that by the most important definition of love that they have - that the world or (often) the church has - they are unloved. The word "single" means they have not found anyone willing to love them. To make matters worst, many of your singles have also suffered incredible rejection from parents or ex-spouses. Be very careful telling them they are loved. Nothing you can say will convince them and the message is sometimes perceived as phony, even when well meant.

Of course, it is a lie because God does love them. But words will never overcome that lie; they need actions. They need to see in concrete visible ways that God's family as individuals knows them and values them enough to love them as individuals. This takes a lot of time and, well, just plain Love.

Stealth Dating

The term "Stealth Dating" actually is used for two distinct phenomena. Both are sins which can trip up godly Christian singles.

The first is the practice of a couple dating for a long period (sometimes 6-12 months) and keeping it secret from even their closest friends. It is common not to advertise a relationship during the first month or so while a couple figures out if it is something serious, but this form of stealth dating continues the secrecy for much longer in a furtive and deceitful manner. This is very literally just the grade school behavior of "I'll be your boy/girl-friend as long as you don't tell anyone..." all grown up.

While they justify it in a number of ways, the real reason for this behavior is that one or both sides want to keep their options open in case someone better comes along. They would never admit this, of course. But it betrays a fundamental lack of respect for the other party. It is difficult to develop a healthy relationship while telegraphing that you don't wish to commit even temporarily to the other person.

This kind of stealth dating generally works itself out in one way or another within a year or so. While a sin, it is so self-defeating that it isn't as serious as the other "stealth dating".

In the second form of "stealth dating", a couple are best friends and share everything except marriage vows together. They share their lives, their hobbies, and their weekends and holidays. Their families know them on a first name basis. They may even vacation together, making a big deal of separate rooms, of course (because no matter how it appears to others, there is no hanky-panky going on here; it is a sin of emotional and spiritual fornication, not of physical lust).

This form of stealth dating is sad because it tends to afflict the most godly and mature Christian singles. C.S. Lewis and Dietrich Bonhoeffer both fell into it. Sooner or later it comes apart, and leaves shattered hearts similar to a divorce after adultery.

The lucky ones end after only two or three years. But sometimes it lasts for a decade or more and at the end one party is left with nothing except "might have beens". Yet it is so pernicious because it is so easy to justify. "It's innocent!" The other party is always free to date someone else because they're not a "couple". Except, of course, that in reality they are, and they aren't free.

Teaching Singles

What about the meat market?

The biggest concern of all elders and other Christian leaders about a singles ministry is the fear that it will become a "meat market" where visitors are immediately pounced upon by members of the opposite sex and all social interest revolves around the potential for romance. This is not an unwarranted concern. All Christian singles ministries seem to gain that reputation, deserved or not.

If the leadership of the congregation is not prepared to accept that, then you may as well not bother even starting a singles ministry. But a healthy singles ministry can be the safest place your singles experience, and have informal peer-enforced guidelines on appropriate male-female interaction. ...And it will still have that "meat market" reputation.

A singles ministry without a strong and healthy leadership team comprised of the most active and mature singles in the church will almost inevitably become a meat market, and an unhealthy place for newcomers. At this point it may be time to start all over with a new ministry and new leadership group. It isn't even necessary to formally end the old group; it will wilt on the vine if the new group is healthy and exciting.

On the other hand, even the healthiest ministry often gains an unwarranted reputation for being a meat market. There seem to be two reasons for this. First, some people are so sensitive to the opposite sex that they will take even the most innocent of remarks in the wrong way. Second, it is amazing how many people who have never been to a group are eager to believe and pass on what even a casual visit would reveal as absurd rumors.

The leadership team which the church elders put in place will determine the success or failure of the ministry. If they pray together and play together, then it is likely that their devotion will be contagious. One essential sub-ministry is the meet & greet Shepherding team. Guy greeters greet guys and girl greeters greet girls. And leaders know to keep their eyes open and rescue girls (or guys! The meat market definitely works both ways...) from monopolizers. Your guys are eager to be the knights in shining armor; this is their godly appropriate opportunity.

Teaching Singles

You can reduce the chances of a meat-market mentality by actually teaching on basic interpersonal skills (something that a lot of singles are not strong in) and expectations for guy/girl interaction. Many of your singles honestly don't understand how to ask someone out or what to do when someone asks them out. It may seem a simple trivial skill to you, but it is not to them.

The Creepiness Equation

When there is a culture of respect, no one has to fear. Everyone should know the "Creepiness Equation":

$$D >= (A / 2) + 7$$

It means, "Never ask someone out if they are younger than your age divided by two plus seven." If you do the math, you will see that this equation works well for a wide variety of ages. Statistically it also turns out that the pool of potential dating candidates actually gets larger for most of adult life.

It can be a temptation of leadership to make the Creepiness Equation a rule or law of the group. However, as the biographies in this book show, some outstanding Christians have formed positive romantic relationships with people significantly younger than themselves.

The book of Ruth should be one of the key texts for any singles group. It has so much good stuff to say and is one of the few places where God teaches singles in the Bible. Boaz was clearly quite a bit older than Ruth and explicitly says so in Ruth 3:10. But as long as the younger approaches the older, the creepiness equation doesn't need to apply. This covers those Boaz/Ruth times, for if you recall, Ruth was about as explicit with Boaz as can be imagined.

If your singles ministry is divided out by ages, be flexible. Do not be at all hesitant to enforce the age breaks ruthlessly when necessary for the protection of your flock, but also don't be afraid to stretch them if there is no reason to kick someone out. And don't be afraid to take the heat for either decision. All groups age naturally, and both the upper and lower limits for each group will need raised every few years; just start a new group with lower age limits when warranted.

Teaching Singles

Warning: It's your ministry but their family.

One word of warning if you decide to build a singles ministry: Everyone claims their congregation is a big family. But at the end of the day, you go home to your wife and kids. For many of your singles, your church's singles ministry truly is their family. Canceling it or making arbitrary changes in it will be treated with the same reaction as if someone suddenly announces to you that they are taking your spouse away. The singles will fight you every step of the way, and come to hate you for it.

That's not to say that you cannot make changes, or even kill off a class that has outlived its usefulness. But you must do it carefully and with consideration. Often allowing a bad class to just wither on the vine is the easiest solution. But it must be replaced with something better and more dynamic.

Chapter 27: Meddling (Yours)

    ✞ "It may be better to live under robber barons than under omnipotent moral busybodies. The robber baron's cruelty may sometimes sleep, his cupidity may at some point be satiated; but those who torment us for our own good will torment us without end for they do so with the approval of their own conscience. They may be more likely to go to Heaven, yet at the same time likelier to make a Hell of earth." C.S. Lewis, *God in the Dock*, p. 292

Chapters 9 and 10 are entitled "Meddling (Theirs)", and "Meddling (Ours)". The first discusses appropriate ways to handle other people hurting singles by playing matchmaker or treating them like not full adults. The second is about avoiding doing the same with others.

This chapter is the equivalent for pastors and leaders. It is sad, but there are still many churches and organizations that treat singles as less than whole persons, less than "real" adults. The emphasis on marriage is understandable in light of Satan's assault on it over the last thirty years, but in some cases the baby has been thrown out with the bathwater. Some church organizations feel fine intruding on singles' personal lives in ways they wouldn't dream of with married people.

There is nothing in Scripture that even hints at a second-class nature for singles, or of discrimination. To the contrary, 1st Corinthians 7:32-35 implies the contrary: to the extent that God has expressed a view, singleness is the more desired (dare we say "godlier"?) state. You

Meddling (Yours)

probably don't honestly believe that in your heart, but that's alright, neither do most of your singles. It really doesn't matter. It's what Scripture says.

Sometimes, the excuse is given that "singles don't last". That's a nice anecdotal justification for treating some of your sheep differently than the rest, but it isn't backed up by real life. From Paul and Augustine, down through the Christians covered in this book (C. S. Lewis: 35 years of service; Corrie ten Boom: 43 years; Amy Carmichael: 55 years!), singles have been stalwart servants of Christ. Paul actually knew a little something about what he was talking about in 1st Corinthians 7, as did the Holy Spirit. His observation is less commandment than statement of simple fact.

What is usually meant is that "single guys don't last". Mathematically, that's an illusion generated by the combination of many fewer single male Christians to begin with (for reasons we've already covered), and most of the guys getting married within five years or so of getting plugged into service. That doesn't change the fact that those same individuals are still serving, just married.

While some discrimination is official, much more is just "encouragement toward marriage" or "preference for couples" by leaders in a position of authority. Most of your singles already would like to get married. Trying to please someone else is a _really_ bad reason to get married and generally leads to disaster.

If they hook up with another Christian and want to get married, that's great! Encourage them in it. If they don't, and just seek to serve in your organization as a faithful Christian, that's great, too! Encourage that, as well.

Paul points out that singles can do a lot more undivided service than married people. Make use of these singles God keeps throwing in your path. They are a fertile source not only of evangelism, but also of solid Christian workers.

At one major Bible translation organization which is growing rapidly, 48% of its recruits between 2007 and 2009 were single. That's an even higher percentage than the general population (42%), and dwarfs the

Meddling (Yours)

percentage of singles at most congregations and missions agencies. They've tapped into a vast unreached pool of recruits, and their growth rates (13% per year!) reflect it.

The organization's secret? Just treating singles like any other adult, and not having silly discriminatory rules. And yes, most of the rules surrounding singles in less inviting organizations really are silly.

Treating singles as adults, not long-lived teenagers does not, however, mean not leading them or giving them wise counsel. Singles sometimes struggle with living like adults. Don't let them get away with perpetual post-adolescence. Treat them like grown-ups and expect them to order their lives like adults.

It is true that a single needs less to live on than a couple with children, but there are limits. Discourage them from just renting a room from a family, or not having a car, or any of the other tricks they sometimes use to avoid doing the hard interpersonal work of raising support or simply getting a real job. A 30-something should not be living in a dorm. Tell them to get a life!

Conclusion: Lead your sheep!

As a leader and pastor in the local church or Christian organization, God has given you sheep to shepherd. Some of them are different than many of the others. Your single sheep want to be led. There are also a lot of single sheep wandering around lost and alone that would love to be part of your flock, if they only knew they were welcome. Lead your sheep!

Appendix B: Study Guide

This is an unusual multimedia study. The singles we have read about lived such interesting lives that several of them have been made into movies!

What you will need: A subscription to NetFlix or another movie rental service is not required but is a big help!

Movies In The Study

Shadowlands (C. S. Lewis)

The Hiding Place (Betsie & Corrie ten Boom)

The Story of Amy Carmichael and the Dohnavur Fellowship

Bonhoeffer: Agent of Grace

Shadowlands (C. S. Lewis)

Opening Scene

Is the cricket game of life passing you by?

The Plot Thickens

Read Matthew 25:14-30. "Jack plays safe. He always has." Who said it? What did he mean?

Jack decides to have "The Talk" with Joy and get everything out into the open. Did it really fool her? Did it really fool him?

Was Jack and Joy's relationship healthy before the civil marriage? What about afterward? Do you know any singles who have been best friends for a long time, but nothing more? Are their relationships healthy?

What do you think would have happened if Jack had broken off his friendship with Joy?

> *Popcorn Break!*
>
> Hollywood didn't mention that C. S. Lewis was an animal lover and The Kilns was often overrun with cats and dogs. In addition to animals that he "inherited", Jack had his own dog, a boxer named Ricky.
>
> In his chapter on animals in *The Problem of Pain*, Lewis wrote, "I have been warned not even to raise the question of animal immortality, lest I find myself 'in company with all the old maids'. I have no objection to the company. I do not think either virginity or old age contemptible, and some of the shrewdest minds I have met inhabited the bodies of old maids."

Climax

What did it take to force Jack to admit his love for Joy?

Joy's cancer went into unexpected remission when she was thought just days from death. Many of C. S. Lewis's fans counted it miraculous at the time. Joy had been given some of the first chemotherapy drugs. Does that make it any less miraculous?

Is it better to have loved and lost, or to have never love at all?

How do you help someone who is grieving?

Is it wrong to have serious questions or doubts about God?

Credits

Jack asks Warren, "If you were God and you had created man and woman, what would you do? Let them love each other, and then lose each other? Or keep them safe from both the love and the pain?"

Warren answers, "I'd let them choose for themselves." After Jack agrees, Warren asks, "Do you wish you'd chosen differently?"

Later, Jack tells Douglas, "It doesn't seem fair, does it? If you want the love, you have to have the pain."

Jack has always played it safe. Can he really play it safe? Can we? What would our lives look like if we stopped playing it safe?

The Hiding Place (Betsie & Corrie ten Boom)

Opening Scene

The most extraordinary thing that Corrie did prior to the war was becoming the first licensed female watchmaker in Holland. What is the most extraordinary thing you have done so far?

The Plot Thickens

Early in the movie, Corrie cries, "I hate them." Betsie's response is "Oh, Corrie, you can't hate anyone and walk with the Lord." We know it's wrong to hate; have you ever thought to yourself, "I don't hate so-and-so, I just really dislike them."? Are you fooling God? Are you fooling yourself?

If Betsie and Corrie had never done anything "special" during the war, would their lives have still been used by God?

In search after search, Corrie's Bible is missed through a long strings of coincidences. How have you seen God work through divine providence?

Popcorn Break!

Read Isaiah 53:3-8.

We often look with horror at Nazi Germany and think such a thing could never happen in the United States. Surely not here, Lord!

The protestant Church played a key role in Hitler's initial election. Many Christians viewed him as a counterbalance to god-less communism.

What did you do when America started torturing people?

Does the previous question upset you? Why? Is the question really unjustified?

Climax

"He [God] has power.
Surely he could stop them. Unless, of course, he's a sadist."

"Oh, no, he's love. All love!"

"Then he's impotent. You can't have it both ways my dear."

"We cannot answer. All I can say is that the same God that you are accusing came and lived in the midst of our world. He was beaten and he was mocked, and he died on a cross. And he did it for love... for us."

"And why do you think your God of love sent you here?"

"To obey him. If you know him you don't have to know why."

How do Betsie and Corrie make sense of God's presence in Ravensbruck? How can we make sense of the tragedies and evils in our own lives?

Clerical error! One died while the other went free. Why? Or were they both freed?

Credits

The only good in Ravensbruck concentration camp came from the Christians caught there. God didn't protect Betsie and Corrie. He sent them into harm's way, to rescue those who otherwise would have died without knowing his love. He cared enough to send his very best.

Some of us have been hanging on to hate for a long, long time. It can seem impossible to let it go. Corrie prayed, "Lord, I cannot let go of it. Take this hate out of my life and put your love in its place. Jesus, there are many things I do not understand. Do not let me go mad, poking about on my own. You know what I am. Savior, hide me in the center of your love."

Do you need to pray this prayer with Corrie?

The Story of Amy Carmichael
and the Dohnavur Fellowship

Opening Scene

Sometimes God uses small tasks to prepare us for larger roles. The servant's heart that Amy learns ministering to poor "shawly" women becomes the same heart she uses for 55 years on the mission field. Has God given you any "shawlies"?

The Plot Thickens

The established western missionaries are aghast that Amy would save children from child prostitution. Legally the temples are the children's guardians. Technically, her work falls into a very gray area. Is she right to take such action even if it isn't legal?

The movie glosses over Amy's sojourn in Japan. In fact, she becomes both physically sick and depressed. She returns to England in failure. Like John Mark, she learns from her failure and goes on to many years of service. How do you think the Japanese failure prepares her for success in India?

Popcorn Break!

When she was little, Amy Carmichael prayed for God to change her brown hair to blond, but He never did. Later, it is much easier for her to sneak into temples as a brunette than if she was blond. Thank God for unanswered prayers! What is a prayer you earnestly prayed that you're now glad God didn't answer affirmatively?

Read 1 Corinthians 12:12-31. Dohnavur Fellowship has not remained static. It now has doctors and computer experts, as well as cooks, school teachers, and calligraphers. Sometimes it seems like as singles, we don't have anything to contribute to the Kingdom. What is your gift? How are you using it to serve the Church?

Climax

Read 2 Corinthians 4:7-12. Amy is confined to bed for many years. Does she let this stop her? How can we serve even though we are jars of clay?

Amy can be a firebrand and sometimes difficult to get along with. Today, we might call some of her behavior bipolar. How do you think that impacts her ministry?

Credits

Read Mark 10:28-30. Like many singles, Amy struggles with loneliness. How does she see this fulfilled in her own life? Are you seeing it fulfilled in your life?

Bonhoeffer: Agent of Grace

Opening Scene

Dietrich refuses to speak at his twin sister's Jewish father-in-law's funeral. He also flees, first to Britain and Spain, then to America. How do you think these early failures influence his later actions?

Describe a time when you failed to take a stand. What did you learn from it?

The Plot Thickens

All members of the armed forces are required to take a loyalty oath specifically to Adolf Hitler, and most other members of society are strongly pressured to take it. Oaths are taken seriously in German culture. How might this cause additional struggles for the plotters?

Dietrich says that the oath is incompatible with Christianity because Hitler requires total commitment, something only Christ can command of a Christian. Can we accept that claim from any person, nation, or cause except Jesus?

Could you give a blessing to a suicide bomber?

> *Popcorn Break!*
>
> Bishop George Bell was one of the foremost Anglican churchmen, and a close friend of Dietrich. He was widely expected to be the next Archbishop of Canterbury. Before the war, he was a staunch opponent of Nazism.
>
> During the war he moderated his stance and opposed bombing of civilians, so the Gestapo would view him as unsuspicious when he met Dietrich as a courier. He was reviled by many English because of his perceived change of heart, and passed over for the Archbishop's position.
>
> Bishop Bell passed the British government detailed information about the plots to kill Hitler, but they were committed to "unconditional surrender" and refused to assist the resistance.
>
> Afterwards, most people who could have exonerated him were dead. George Bell died before his name was cleared.

The events related to Dietrich's fiance, Maria von Wedemeyer, portrayed in the movie, actually take place over a number of years. What are some of the problems when a couple have a significant age difference?

The world would consider Dietrich and Maria's relationship very romantic, but utterly a failure. Their love is never consummated. He is executed and years later she eventually marries another. In the grand scheme of things, what is the point?

Climax

There is a vast difference between the stereotypical concentration camp and how an upper-class German from an influential family is treated in prison.

The Gestapo and SS are deeply involved in looting fleeing Jews, and for a long time, they think Dietrich's main crime is simply corruption. Because they are corrupt, they assume he is in some way profiting from helping Jews escape.

Read Romans 13:1-2. Satan can quote Scripture. Continue reading v3-7. How do you think the latter verses clarify the first two verses? What would Dietrich say about v5?

In the movie, Dietrich says, "Consider this... If a teacher asks a boy in front of the whole class if his father came home drunk again the night before, is the boy obligated to answer 'yes'?" The guard responds, "No." and Dietrich continues, "Exactly. The teacher is abusing his power in asking that question. The honest answer is for the boy to lie, defending his father and lie, for all he's worth."

Dietrich is not advocating situational ethics in the sense meant by some. The movie is attempting to portray his views on Romans 13:7. Dietrich actually says very little to his interrogator, remaining silent whenever possible. When he must speak, he tells the truth, as briefly and minimally as possible. How would you handle such an interrogation?

Credits

Flossenburg is known as the execution camp where Hitler's political enemies are sent to be killed. Life in Germany towards the end of WWII widely assumes a circus-like quality. The entire final farce portrayed in the movie actually occurs: the charcoal-fueled prison van, the bizarre bus-ride, the imprisonment in the church/school, and finally the execution just days before liberation. Captured British "not-so-secret" service officer, Payne Best, survives to describe it all, and to bring Dietrich's last words to Bishop George Bell.

As Dietrich is stripped naked and hanged, he has come a long way from the man who was scared to preach at his sister's Jewish father-in-law's funeral. He marches right up to the scaffold, and into Paradise.

Dietrich was deeply concerned with "cheap grace", the message that grace does not require anything from the recipient. What do you think Dietrich would say to the Church today?

About the Author

Stephen Fierbaugh has been celibate for over a decade and has no children. He is a missionary with Pioneer Bible Translators, taking care of the organization's computer needs and making sure that the missionaries get their spam.

Stephen may be contacted at <stephen@fierbaugh.org>. He is available for speaking engagements.

www.ingramcontent.com/pod-product-compliance
Lightning Source LLC
Chambersburg PA
CBHW032122090426
42743CB00007B/430